TRACING YOUR
HUGUENOT
ANCESTORS

FAMILY HISTORY FROM PEN & SWORD

Tracing Your Channel Islands Ancestors
Marie-Louise Backhurst

Tracing Your Yorkshire Ancestors
Rachel Bellerby

Tracing Your Royal Marine Ancestors
Richard Brooks and Matthew Little

Tracing Your Pauper Ancestors
Robert Burlison

Tracing Your Labour Movement Ancestors
Mark Crail

Tracing Your Army Ancestors
Simon Fowler

A Guide to Military History on the Internet
Simon Fowler

Tracing Your Northern Ancestors
Keith Gregson

Your Irish Ancestors
Ian Maxwell

Tracing Your Scottish Ancestors
Ian Maxwell

Tracing Your London Ancestors
Jonathan Oates

Tracing Your Tank Ancestors
Janice Tait and David Fletcher

Tracing Your Air Force Ancestors
Phil Tomaselli

Tracing Your Secret Service Ancestors
Phil Tomaselli

Tracing Your Criminal Ancestors
Stephen Wade

Tracing Your Police Ancestors
Stephen Wade

Tracing Your Jewish Ancestors
Rosemary Wenzerul

Fishing and Fishermen
Martin Wilcox

Tracing Your Canal Ancestors
Sue Wilkes

TRACING YOUR HUGUENOT ANCESTORS

A Guide for Family Historians

Kathy Chater

Pen & Sword
FAMILY HISTORY

First published in Great Britain in 2012 by
PEN & SWORD FAMILY HISTORY
an imprint of
Pen & Sword Books Ltd
47 Church Street
Barnsley
South Yorkshire
S70 2AS

ISBN 978 1 84884 610 4

A CIP catalogue record for this book is
available from the British Library.

Typeset in Palatino and Optima by
Phoenix Typesetting, Auldgirth, Dumfriesshire

Printed and bound in England by
CPI Group (UK) Ltd, Croydon, CR0 4YY

Pen & Sword Books Ltd incorporates the imprints of
Pen & Sword Aviation, Pen & Sword Family History, Pen & Sword Maritime,
Pen & Sword Military, Pen & Sword Discovery, Wharncliffe Local History,
Wharncliffe True Crime, Wharncliffe Transport, Pen & Sword Select, Pen &
Sword Military Classics, Leo Cooper, The Praetorian Press, Remember When,
Seaforth Publishing and Frontline Publishing

For a complete list of Pen & Sword titles please contact
PEN & SWORD BOOKS LIMITED
47 Church Street, Barnsley, South Yorkshire, S70 2AS, England
E-mail: enquiries@pen-and-sword.co.uk
Website: www.pen-and-sword.co.uk

CONTENTS

INTRODUCTION

In today's secular society it is difficult to understand the crucial role that religion played in the past in Europe. For centuries wars were fought which resulted in regions changing rulers, each imposing different religious orthodoxies on the inhabitants. This resulted in massive migrations of people, both within Europe and across the Atlantic to the Americas, because their beliefs mattered so much to them. Between the sixteenth and eighteenth centuries, the biggest group of what would today be called asylum seekers were Protestants, generally known as Huguenots.

The derivation of the term Huguenot is not really known, although it may be from the German *Eidgenossen* (confederates bound together by oath), used between 1520 and 1524 for the people of Geneva in Switzerland who opposed the Duke of Savoy. One of their leaders was called Besançon Hugues and this may have influenced the name. Another possibility is that the term is derived from the French *Huguon* meaning one who walks by night: Protestants in Catholic countries had to conceal themselves from the authorities and took to holding services at night in isolated places.

Strictly speaking, Huguenots are those who fled from France in the time of Louis XIV (reigned 1643–1715) because of religious persecution. The Huguenot Society decided at the outset to include in its remit earlier Protestant refugees who had left the Low Countries and France in the sixteenth century. The Low Countries consisted of present-day Netherlands; Flanders, a region now in Northern France but then in the Spanish-ruled Netherlands; present-day Belgium and Luxembourg. The southern part of this area was inhabited by French-speakers, called Walloons, and those from the northern part were Dutch-speaking. I have decided to include all three groups – Dutch, Walloons and Huguenots – in this work, partly because they have their religion in common and partly because they are all often referred to as Huguenots.

Before 1752, the new year began on 25 March so dates between 1 January and 24 March are usually written 2 January 1700/1 or whatever to avoid confusion between the practice then and now. However in Scotland and mainland Europe, the change had generally taken place in 1600 so family historians need to be aware of this when doing research.

The Huguenot Society

The Huguenot Society of London was founded in 1885 to promote the publication and interchange of knowledge about Huguenots in the United Kingdom. It is not limited to those with Huguenot ancestry, but is also open to those who are interested in the subject. In 1986 it became the Huguenot Society of Great Britain and Ireland to reflect the breadth of interests among the Society's membership. As well as holding four meetings a year in London, where a paper on an aspect of Huguenot history is given, the Society arranges occasional visits to places of interest in the United Kingdom and overseas. There have also been conferences, such as 'From Strangers to Citizens', held in 2000 to commemorate the 450th anniversary of Edward VI's charter allowing 'strangers' to set up their own churches. The Society also has an extensive programme of publishing: as well as the *Proceedings of the Huguenot Society*, containing articles and book reviews, there is the Huguenot Society Quarto Series (HSQS), volumes of transcriptions of church registers and associated documents, like the archives of the French Hospital, and editions of historic works such as a contemporary account of the religious war in the Cévennes region of France by Abraham and Elie Marion. The new series has reprints of autobiographies of various refugees and academic studies of particular topics, like the history of the French Church in Southampton. The Society's publications, listed in the Bibliography, and its Library are the primary sources of information about Huguenots in Britain.

The Irish Section of the Society was set up in 1986. It holds an annual service at St Patrick's Cathedral in Dublin each November, and also arranges lectures and visits.

Acknowledgements

I have drawn heavily from articles in the *Proceedings of the Huguenot Society* and the Huguenot Society's other published works, especially the registers of the various churches, which usually give a detailed account of the church's history. Together these sources contain a formidable body of expertise. The various writers are too numerous to list but I am in grateful awe of their knowledge and scholarship, which I have necessarily had to abridge for this publication. Researchers should follow up the various works listed in the Bibliography. I would also like to thank Lucy Gwynn, the Librarian of the Huguenot Library, for her unstinting help and for generously sharing her extensive knowledge of the archives.

Abbreviations

HSQS	Huguenot Society Quarto Series
Proceedings	*Proceedings of the Huguenot Society*
HL	Huguenot Library (in London)
GL	Guildhall Library
LMA	London Metropolitan Archives
PCC	Prerogative Court of Canterbury
TNA	The National Archives

Picture Credits

Images pp. 10, 65, 85, 87 courtesy of the Huguenot Library; pp.11, 122 courtesy of Wikicommons; p. 108 photograph taken by Jim Linwood; pp. 110, 111 courtesy of the German Huguenot Museum. All other images are from the author's collection.

Chapter 1

THE HISTORY OF THE HUGUENOTS

When ex-monk Martin Luther (1483–1546) nailed his ninety-five theses to the church door in Wittenberg in 1517, he intended to reform the Roman Catholic Church. Instead he sparked a revolution that split Europe and the effects of which are still felt today. Many people all over the continent had long been unhappy with the corruption that had crept into the all-powerful Church's practices and wanted to return to Biblical teachings.

The other major figure involved in the spread of ideas about reforming the Church was Jean Calvin (1509–64), a French theologian who fled to Switzerland when his inflammatory preachings put his life in danger in his homeland.

The followers of Luther and Calvin became known as Protestants and the change from Catholicism to Protestantism is called the Reformation. It was not just a religious movement: the questioning of the Church's authority inevitably led to the examination of the power (or abuse of it) of the temporal rulers who were supported by and closely linked with the Church.

This is not the place to examine in detail the many theological differences which led to such devastating consequences but an awareness of the religious tensions that existed both between Protestants and Catholics and between the different branches of Protestantism is necessary for those

Martin Luther (1483–1546)

1

*Jean Calvin
(1509–64)*

tracing their ancestry. People's beliefs at that time were sometimes literally a matter of life and death. Various factors were also the cause of intense disputes within Protestantism and theological differences caused debates within the French Protestant churches, at times splitting them, causing individuals to leave, either for other congregations or even for other denominations. It is hard in our secular times to understand the dominant position that religion occupied in the lives of a large part of the population before the twentieth century.

Catholicism and Protestantism

There were major differences between these two branches of Christianity. Roman Catholicism had a hierarchy with the Pope at the apex because he was regarded as the successor to St Peter, the most important of Christ's apostles whom God appointed as the head of His church. God could only

2

be approached through the clergy, the Pope's representatives, or by prayers to the Virgin Mary and the other saints, asking them to intervene with God on the supplicant's behalf. Protestants regarded the Pope simply as the Bishop of Rome and said that lay people could communicate directly with God. They did not condone the adoration of saints. Protestants also rejected transubstantiation, the Catholic belief that at the moment of communion the bread and wine turned into the actual body and blood of Christ. Protestants said that communion was a commemoration of a single event that had happened once in the past and which was not repeated.

Another important difference was the way individuals could achieve the salvation of their souls. Catholics said this was through works, such as purchasing indulgences in order to atone for their own sins or by paying for masses to be said for the souls of the deceased to lessen their time in purgatory. Protestants said that faith alone was justification and that prayers should be said only for the living, not for the dead.

The Catholic Church used only the Bible in Latin, which restricted the reading of it to a small, educated elite. Protestants believed that individuals were responsible for their own salvation, as this required understanding of the faith to which they subscribed. Therefore they had translations made into local languages so that people could read the Bible for themselves. Protestants also laid much more emphasis on the Old Testament than Catholics did.

However, within Protestantism there were many divisions. Catholicism had a magisterium, a body of accepted teachings which could only be modified by edicts from the Pope. The Protestant emphasis on the individual's interpretation of the Bible and theology in general meant that there were constant debates about even minor points of doctrine. Calvin's form of Protestantism was stricter than Luther's and, very broadly speaking, the two branches epitomise the essential divide among Protestants. Lutheranism accepted a hierarchy of authority within the Church, represented by bishops and archbishops. The Calvinists had individual congregations governed only by elders of equal rank. A smaller group of Protestants, known as Anabaptists, did not believe in infant baptism. As genealogists get a great deal of information from the baptismal records of children (parents' names, place of residence, dates when a family was resident), anabaptist ancestors cause major problems in this respect.

From the early days of Protestantism in England there were people who wanted a more radical reform of the Church than the government was prepared to make. The Church of England retained bishops and archbishops but the more fundamental Protestants, who became known as Puritans, wanted to do away with this hierarchy and devolve power down to individual congregations. They were initially called Separatists, later becoming the Congregationalists. The history of dissent from the Anglican

3

brand of Protestantism is a long story of splits and the establishment of numerous denominations and sects. The Baptists, for example, were founded in 1611 by a Separatist who had studied in Amsterdam, and they do not practise infant baptism. The all-purpose term for non-Anglicans was Independents but the term Dissenters is now generally applied to three denominations descended from the Separatists: the Congregationalists, the Baptists and the English Presbyterians. It was not until the middle of the nineteenth century that boundaries between these non-conforming movements became more rigid.

Europe in the Reformation

Family historians need to have a basic understanding of the geography of Europe and the factors which caused migrants to leave one place for another at a particular period so that they can track their ancestors' movements and where the documents relating to them might be found.

The collection of islands that make up the British Isles have an obviously fixed and easily defended boundary, the sea, so were relatively united. Mainland Europe, however, had fewer natural borders. Some of the present-day countries in Europe did not exist. Germany and Italy, for example, were not united until 1871 and 1861 respectively (and there were still a couple of Italian provinces which did not join until later). At that time much of mainland Europe might be better understood as an assortment of provinces. In records, those arriving from overseas give the name of the region from which they came rather than the country in which it was situated. Territories on the borders of powerful nations, like Flanders, Lorraine and Alsace, today within France, might change hands as the result of wars, treaties and marriage alliances.

Religion and politics were inextricably bound together. They dominated the sixteenth and seventeenth centuries and led to both civil and national wars across Europe. Some of the rulers were intellectually convinced by Protestantism but for others the reformed religion was a form of political protest, especially in the German states.

The majority of the aristocracy remained loyal to Catholicism. Protestantism seems to have appealed mainly to the middle classes and skilled artisans – people used to running their own businesses and lives and resentful of interference with their autonomy – and to the rural peasantry. However, peasants did not often have the means to escape and in most countries conformed to Catholicism.

The Holy Roman Empire was a major force until 1806. It centred on Austria and was ruled by the Catholic Habsburg family. Through centuries of successful warfare and strategic marriages they had emerged as the monarchs of a large part of Europe, in which they continued to play a significant role until 1806. During the period covered by this book, the

4

Holy Roman Empire also governed many of the southern German territories, Hungary, Bohemia (part of present-day Czech Republic), Silesia (now part of Poland), Serbia and Croatia. Another branch, the Spanish Habsburgs, ruled the Low Countries from 1549. Despite its apparent omnipotence, there were differences in how the Church was administered under different rulers and the Spanish monarchy had introduced some reforms in Spain and the territories it controlled, although the establishment of the feared Inquisition there in 1483 enforced conformity through torture, the burning of heretics at the stake and the confiscation of their property. There were therefore very few Spanish Protestants.

The upheavals in continental Europe resulted in long, vicious wars of religion, which created numerous refugees (the word is French in origin and originated with the Huguenots). The economic problems that wars brought added to their numbers. Again, this is too complex a subject to discuss in detail but family historians tracing their ancestry in sixteenth-, seventeenth- and eighteenth-century Europe need a broad understanding of events in the different regions in order to pinpoint where their ancestors might have come from and when and where they might have migrated to at any particular time. In 1689, for example, the entire congregation of the Walloon church in Mannheim, Germany, decided to relocate to Magdeburg, some 230 miles away.

Germany

Until unification, Germany, where the Reformation started, was a collection of over 300 states and statelets. Some, like Brandenburg, Saxony and Bavaria were comparatively substantial. Others were counties, like Munster or the Duchy of Westphalia, and there were numerous city-states, like Bremen. Some areas were under ecclesiastical control, like the Bishopric of Passau. Due to territorial conquests and marriage alliances, individual rulers might control more than one place. Both the Austrian and Spanish Habsburgs controlled many of the regions. Others banded together to protect their own interests, like the Wetterau Association. The first stirrings of the Reformation were in East Friesland, just north of the Netherlands, in 1520, and spread out to other regions.

There were, as elsewhere, different branches of Protestantism. Some regions chose the Lutheran model, others the Reformed (Calvinist). A few, such as the Palatinate, started out Lutheran but later took the Reformed path. Nor was it always a simple choice between two alternatives. Martin Bucer, a contemporary of Martin Luther, was influential, especially in Hesse, and the Swiss Ulrich Zwingli also had followers.

Across this patchwork of places, religious and political conflict raged. The small size of many of the German regions meant that the rulers had greater control over their populations' beliefs and in 1555 the Treaty of

Augsburg resolved that a state's official religion would be determined by its ruler. When the ruler changed, the official religion might also change although many of the inhabitants often resisted conversion so this did not put an end to religious conflict.

It would be too long and confusing a task to detail the effects on each and every separate territory but the County of Lingen provides a good example. From 1496 it had come under the rule of the Count of Tecklenburg. Konrad of Tecklenburg introduced Lutheranism in 1541. In 1578 it came under the rule of the House of Orange, who were convinced Calvinists, and the Prince brought in his brand of reformation from 1597. Lingen was then conquered by the Spanish in 1605 and Catholicism imposed. The territory was reconquered in 1633 by the Dutch House of Orange who restored Calvinism. This time the population rebelled: they wanted to remain Catholic and were prepared to cross boundaries to attend forbidden services. From 1702 the County of Lingen belonged to Prussia but the official Church language and services remained Dutch into the nineteenth century. And this pattern of expecting the ruled to fall in with the current ruler's faith was repeated elsewhere; Lingen is just one example.

The Thirty Years War

Between 1618 and 1648 the Thirty Years War devastated Germany. It was fought on religious grounds between the Protestant rulers, supported by Denmark and Sweden, against the Habsburgs. France, in the interests of weakening Spanish and Austrian rule in Europe, joined in on the Protestant side, while trying to stamp out Protestantism in its own lands. It is estimated that in total Germany lost over half its population: in some places up to 70 per cent died. It was not until the Treaty of Westphalia was signed in 1648 that the disputes ended and brought official recognition of Protestantism.

The Low Countries

Protestants left their homelands in two waves. The first influx of refugees, overwhelmingly Calvinists or Anabaptists, came from the mid-sixteenth century onwards mainly from the Low Countries, an area with a complicated history. The Low Countries (a literal translation of Nederlands) consisted of seventeen provinces: the counties of Artois and Flanders (now in Northern France); the Duchy of Luxembourg and numerous smaller regions, which form the present-day Netherlands, Belgium and Luxembourg. One of these smaller territories was the province of Holland, where the major cities of Amsterdam, Rotterdam and The Hague are situated. It is common to call the present-day Netherlands 'Holland' but this is an error: it is just one province of the country.

The Low Countries in the late sixteenth century

In general the southern part of this region (Wallonia) was French-speaking, having been ruled by the Kingdom of France; the northern area, the region of Flanders, was part of the Holy Roman Empire. The inhabitants here spoke Flemish, closely related to Dutch. In 1830 the country of Belgium was created but the two groups still retain their separate languages and cultures.

Trading links between the Low Countries and Germany and Switzerland brought the ideas of the reformed Protestant religion, which was strongly resisted by devoutly Catholic Spain. The Inquisition was re-introduced into the Low Countries in 1522 and the first Protestant martyr in the region was burned at the stake a year later. Between 1529 and 1550 various edicts were issued, bringing in the death penalty for Lutherans, possession of a Protestant Bible or other works, or for attending a

7

Protestant church service. Philip, son of Charles V, the Holy Roman Emperor, was proclaimed King of Spain in 1556, when the Reformation had built up serious momentum, and he set about bringing orthodoxy to his Low Country territories. They had remained a loosely linked confederation with a degree of local autonomy and privileges while under Spanish rule and they were often at loggerheads with each other, but in 1559 the northern Dutch provinces united against Spain. In 1562 Philip II of Spain sent the Duke of Alva to enforce restrictions against Protestants and the severities he introduced triggered a wave of migrants. Hostilities continued until 1606, when a truce was declared. Although ruled by Catholic Spain until 1713 and then until 1794 by Catholic Austria, the Dutch had effectively won their independence. They retained their Republic, known as the United Provinces, and its official religion was the Reformed Church. The southern provinces remained loyal to Spain and Catholicism.

France

France, territorially smaller than it is today, was comparatively united by the end of the sixteenth century. Jean Calvin (originally Jean Chauvin) was born in 1507 in Noyon in the north, which remained a strongly Catholic region. Protestantism took hold mainly in the south, where there was also an element of political protest in its rise. The first refugees from the Low Countries were augmented by those fleeing France.

Refugees from France

Between 1652 and 1698 the French Wars of Religion were fought between Catholics and Protestants. Migrants left France throughout the whole period of the wars, but a major exodus followed the Massacre of St Bartholomew, an uprising against Protestants in France, which began on 23 August 1572. The original aim seems to have been to assassinate just a few important Protestants in Paris but it got out of hand. When the bloodshed finished in October, an estimated 10,000 people had been slaughtered, initially in Paris, but then spreading into strongholds of Protestantism, especially in the south. Pope Gregory XIII issued a medal celebrating the event.

It is virtually impossible to calculate the numbers who left their countries during this first wave. A number of them returned to their homeland in the first half of the seventeenth century, when the situation there improved following the Edict of Nantes (1598), which granted Protestants a degree of toleration on condition that they did not try to convert others to their beliefs. This is seen as the end of the wars, but there was still some residual rebellion and conflicts thereafter. Some historians put the end of

1	Flanders (from 1659, previously Spanish Netherlands)	20	Marche
2	Artois (from 1659, previously Spanish Netherlands)	21	Bourbonnais
		22	Saintonge
		23	Augumois
3	Picardy	24	Guyenne
4	Normandy	25	Limousin
5	Île de France	26	Auvergne
6	Champagne	27	Lyonnais
7	Lorraine (from 1737, previously Holy Roman Empire)	28	Savoie (from 1697, previously Holy Roman Empire)
8	Bretagne/Brittany	29	Dauphiné
9	Maine	30	Gascogne/Gascony
10	Orleanais	31	Languedoc
11	Alsace (from 1639, previously Holy Roman Empire)	32	Comtat Venaissin (papal enclave until 1791)
12	Anjou	33	Provence
13	Touraine	34	Comté de Nice (under protection of Savoy)
14	Berry		
15	Nivernais	35	Béarn
16	Burgogne/Burgundy	36	Comté de Foix
17	Franche Comté (from 1678, previously Spanish Habsburg)	37	Roussillon
18	Poitou		Note: France also ruled the island of Corsica in the Mediterranean.
19	Aunis		

The ancient provinces of France

the religious wars as late as 1629. The families who went back after 1598 must have not long returned before legal discrimination against them in France resurfaced. Henri IV, who had promoted the Edict, was assassinated in 1610 and his successors were less well disposed towards Protestants. Under Louis XIV (1638–1715) persecution intensified. Between 1660 and 1685 over 300 decrees that discriminated against them were issued and their places of worship were destroyed on increasingly spurious grounds. This started the second wave of refugees. In the century following 1660, between 200,000 and 250,000 Protestants left France.

The majority left after 1681, when the dragonnades were unleashed, in which dragoons (armed cavalry soldiers) were billeted on Huguenot families. They had to be supported at the expense of the people with whom they were lodged and were encouraged to behave cruelly. They were so feared that on the approach of dragoons to a town, the Protestant inhabitants would publicly abjure their faith in droves.

In 1685 the Edict of Nantes was revoked. All Protestant services were banned and ministers forcibly exiled if they would not convert. Men who refused to do so could be sent as slaves to the galleys (the French navy in the Mediterranean used ships that were rowed, as well as driven by sails) or even tortured to death; women might be imprisoned and their children were removed to be raised as Catholics. Ordinary people were not allowed to leave France and could be imprisoned for attempting to do so. Some later

French Protestants held secret services in the open air at night.

wrote accounts of their experiences, like Jean Migault, a pastor in Poitou, or the Reverend Jacques Fontaine. The way they were guided along routes using safe houses resembled that used by Allied airmen shot down in the Second World War in occupied France or the 'underground' railroad that conveyed American slaves to freedom in the nineteenth century. It is argued that it was the start of the dragonnades that caused the biggest exodus. By the time the Edict was revoked, life had become intolerable for Protestants but not all were able to escape immediately: many pretended to covert but bided their time. During the period between 1685 and the individuals' escapes, they attended Catholic churches, because their religion enjoined them to obey lawful authority, and records of the baptisms of their children, their marriages and the burials of their dead will be recorded in the standard Catholic Church records. However, many attended services *au désert* (in the desert, a Biblical allusion to Moses in the wilderness), that is, in secret locations in the open air. Few records of these survive.

By the beginning of the eighteenth century, the flood from France had reduced to a steady stream and finally a trickle. The last emigrants resulted from local outbreaks of persecution between 1745 and 1754 in the Dauphiné, the Cévennes and Languedoc. By 1760, Huguenots had virtually ceased to leave. Anyone migrating between that time and the French Revolution in 1789 would not have done so for religious reasons, but would have been effectively an economic migrant. The French people who fled the Reign of Terror following the Revolution were overwhelmingly Roman Catholic and are not considered as Huguenots: the persecution they were escaping was political, not religious.

The Huguenot Cross

The Huguenot Cross

There are many stories surrounding the origins of the Huguenot Cross. It is said to have been originally designed in Nîmes in the 1680s, at the start of the period of the greatest persecution, but it was not until the nineteenth century that descendants of Huguenot refugees began to wear it, especially in the United States. During the Second World War the Free French Protestants in Britain designed a badge that combined it with the Cross of Lorraine, the symbol of the Free French in general. Today it is incorporated into the logo of the French Reformed Church and appears on buildings connected with this church.

However it originated, it is based on the Order of the Holy Spirit, which Henry VI, who was responsible for the Edict of Nantes, instituted in 1578. It also has elements of the Maltese Cross, which was the badge of the Crusaders and traditionally symbolises protection from fire. The elements carry important meanings: the fleur de lys is the badge of France and the twelve points of the four fleurs de lys stand for the apostles. The heart-shaped gap in the centre commemorates the personal seal of Jean Calvin and also symbolises loyalty. The eight points represent the eight beatitudes (Matthew 5:3–12) and the four petals stand for the four gospels. The dove hanging beneath is the sign of the Holy Spirit. In times of persecution, this could be replaced by a pearl, symbolising tears.

Switzerland

Switzerland, well protected from invaders by its mountainous terrain, was at the time of the Reformation divided into thirteen self-governing cantons, joined in a confederation. Four languages were spoken across the country: French, German, Italian and Romansch.

Ulrich Zwingli, one of the major early Protestant theologians, converted the city council of Zurich in 1523 and the changes introduced there spread to several other important towns. Seven cantons remained Roman Catholic, provoking the Wars of Kappel. The conflict was not as prolonged as religious wars elsewhere and ended in 1531 with the Catholics victorious. Distrust and animosity between the Protestant and Catholic cantons continued. Swiss mercenaries fought in the French Wars of Religion and the Thirty Years War in Germany on both sides. The confederation, however, put aside its religious animosities and remained neutral, so Switzerland was an early place of refuge.

Italy

In the south the Kingdom of Naples was under Habsburg rule and the Papal States in the centre remained Catholic. The few converts to Protestantism here were almost all from the northern regions, primarily Piedmont on the border with Switzerland, where most emigrants moving for religious reasons from Italy went. There was a small Italian Protestant church in London in the late sixteenth century but this was not long-lived. Individuals continued to arrive sporadically in the seventeenth and eighteenth centuries. They usually joined, at least initially, the French churches in London.

Destinations

Most Huguenots who were able to leave were merchants or artisans: they had the means to pay their passage and had skills that they could take with them when they emigrated. They might, therefore, move from one country to another, confident of their abilities to find work. This might happen over one or two generations. Because the northern part of the Netherlands had won a degree of independence from Spanish rule by 1609, it was a destination for many French and Walloon refugees. Others went to the British Isles and to the Protestant German states. Some went directly to North America, others stayed for a while in Britain, the Netherlands or Germany before relocating to North America, the Caribbean colonies or South Africa.

It is, however, important to realise that people have been migrating throughout Europe for centuries. In 1619, for example, James I invited a group of Flemish tapestry weavers to come to Mortlake in South London, where he had established a factory. He recruited them because of their superior skills. Many of those who went to North America and the Caribbean were also escaping poverty to improve their financial prospects. Their motives were economic, to create a better life for themselves and their families.

Timeline

1517 Martin Luther puts forward proposals to reform the Roman Catholic Church, sparking the Reformation.

1533 Jean Calvin flees France for Switzerland.

1534 Henry VIII's Act of Supremacy establishes control of the Church in England.

1535 Edict ordering the extermination of Protestants in France results in emigrations.

1536 In Basel Calvin publishes Institutes of the Christian Religion, detailing his Reformed doctrines, and goes to Geneva.

      In England the Dissolution of the Monasteries ends Catholic influence.

1541 After a period in Strasbourg, Calvin returns to Geneva to establish a church and community based on his teachings.

1547 Edward VI succeeds Henry VIII and brings in a stricter form of Protestantism.

1550 Edward VI grants Huguenot refugees the right to worship in England.

1553   In England the accession of the Catholic Mary I, who marries Philip II of Spain, leads to persecution of Protestants and the exit of many to the Netherlands, the German states and Switzerland.

1555   The Peace of Augsburg gives legal rights to Lutherans in the Holy Roman Empire.
       First consistory of a French Protestant church held in Paris.

1558   Accession of Elizabeth I in England restores Protestantism.

1559   First national synod of French Protestants.

1562   The Wars of Religion in France begin.

1563   Foundation of the Church of England.

1567   The Spanish Duke of Alva brings in repressive rule in the Netherlands.

1568   Dutch begin their revolt against Spanish rule.

1572   Massacre of St Bartholomew in France results in large-scale emigration.

1579   Union of Utrecht unites seven of the northern Dutch provinces to form what becomes the Dutch Republic, with Calvinism as the state religion.

1593   Henry IV of France converts to Catholicism.

1598   Edict of Nantes ends the French Wars of Religion and gives Protestants in France legal toleration.

1609   A twelve-year truce between the Dutch and their Spanish rulers agreed, effectively founding the Dutch Republic.

1610   Assassination of Henry IV of France. Accession of Louis XIII.

1618   Beginning of the Thirty Years War in Europe fought on political and religious grounds, sparked by the spread of Protestantism in Bohemia and Austria within the Catholic Holy Roman Empire. Various states of Germany, as well as Denmark, Spain, Sweden, Poland and France drawn in over the whole period.

1620   Pilgrim Fathers seeking religious freedom leave England to settle in North America.

1621   War between Spain and the Dutch Republic re-ignited on the expiry of the twelve-year truce.

1638   After an attempt to impose the English prayer book, a Covenant is signed by Presbyterians in Scotland to defend and preserve their faith. It becomes the majority religion in Scotland.

1642   Outbreak of the English Civil War, largely on political grounds.

1648   End of the Thirty Years War in Europe, which gives the Dutch full independence from Spain and also legal and political equality to Calvinists and Lutherans in the Holy Roman Empire.

1649   Execution of Charles I and the introduction of Oliver Cromwell's Commonwealth brings Presbyterian influence to English government.

1652   Foundation by the Dutch of the Cape Colony in South Africa.

1660   Restoration of Charles II to the English throne brings back Anglicanism.

1681   Start of the dragonnades in France.

1685   James II, effectively Roman Catholic, succeeds to the English throne.

1685   Revocation of the Edict of Nantes in France.

1688   James II of England deposed. The Dutch William of Orange invited to become King of England, ruling jointly with his wife Mary, James II's daughter.

1690   William III defeats James II at the Battle of the Boyne in Ireland, re-establishing English rule there. Many of his army were of Huguenot origin.

1702   Protestant uprising in the Cévennes in southern France: hostilities last until 1711.

1715   Jacobite rising by the Catholic son of James II, the 'Old Pretender', defeated.
        First synod *au désert* (in the desert) held in Nîmes, showing that Protestantism in France had not been eradicated.

1724   Louis XV increases penalties against Protestants: men to be sent to the galleys for life, women to be imprisoned for life and ministers to be executed. Children of Protestant marriages made illegitimate by law.

1789   During the French Revolution the National Assembly asserts the right of freedom of worship and equal access to civil offices and professions for Protestants.

1802   Full civil and religious equality for French Protestants under the 'Code Napoléon'.

Chapter 2

SETTLEMENTS
IN GREAT BRITAIN

Along with the Netherlands, the British Isles were the most popular destination for Huguenot refugees and in particular England attracted the greatest number. In England the Church of England was effectively established in 1533 and followed the Lutheran model with a hierarchy of power of bishops and archbishops, although there was a strong and influential Calvinist movement, known as the Puritans. In Scotland Presbyterianism, based on the Calvinist model, became predominant. The majority of people in Ireland remained Roman Catholic, but were ruled by English Protestants. Wales had been under English rule since medieval times but in 1536 an Act of Union brought it into the English legal system.

In 1550 Edward VI, an ardent follower of the Reformed religion, granted Protestant refugees the right to worship in their own churches. The Church of Austin Friars in the City of London became known as the Dutch Church. It is still used by Dutch people today. The French-speaking refugees were granted the Chapel and Sacristy of the Hospital of St Anthony by the dean and canons of Windsor in the same year. This became known as the French Church of Threadneedle Street and was the largest and most powerful of the Huguenot churches in England.

It is estimated that there may have been up to 10,000 in the first wave of refugees but how many remained when conditions in their homelands eased is not known. In the Privy Council Proceedings of September 1553, there are warrants to the mayors of Dover and Rye to permit French Protestants lately living in London to pass out of the realm; and in March, 1554, it was positively commanded 'that all foreign refugees, not being denizens [i.e. having been granted the right to live in the country], should depart out of the realm'. It is clear that many did not go. The second wave from France from the 1680s brought between 40,000 and 50,000.

Later, when William of Orange was asked to come to England to become King William III in 1688, many Dutch people and first- and second-generation French refugees living in the Netherlands followed him.

As the map shows, there were no communities in the north of England.

16

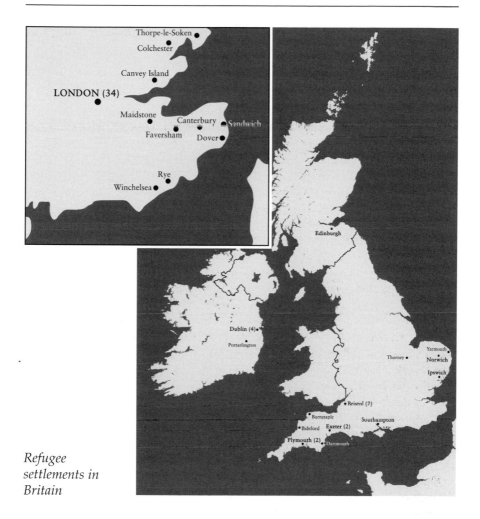

Refugee settlements in Britain

There may have been a small community in Coventry: a minister was given permission to form a congregation there in 1570 and it seems to have been in existence six years later. Any individuals or families who went there or outside the main settlements will be found in the standard genealogical sources.

The primary division between the congregations was whether they conformed to the Anglican Church, with its hierarchy of bishops inherited from Catholicism, or were nonconformist, with independent congregations and elected elders. The Church of England formed part of the government and until the nineteenth century there was discrimination against all religious denominations outside the Church of England. The government wanted the refugees to conform and both gave inducements

17

and applied pressure to encourage this but many religious refugees had suffered too much for their faith to abandon their Calvinist beliefs.

In 1840 the government called in all registers held by non-Anglican churches. There was a good response but a further Act was passed in 1858 because not all had been given in. The Huguenot churches, including those that conformed to Anglicanism, surrendered their registers and they are now in The National Archives (TNA). They are also available online. Details of baptisms and marriages have been extracted by the Church of Latter-Day Saints and included in the International Genealogical Index (IGI) on their website. This, however, has only names, dates and places, it does not include additional information, like godparents and addresses. The surviving registers of the Huguenot churches have been published by the Huguenot Society (HS) and are all available on CD-ROM, including the church in Dover's registers, which were privately published in 1888. The exceptions are the registers of the Dutch church in Norwich, which is now held in London Metropolitan Archives (LMA), and the Dutch Church at Austin Friars in London, also in LMA. Transcriptions of the latter's registers up to 1853 have been published.

Only some of the churches had burial grounds, so the registers usually include just baptisms and marriages. Following the 1753 Marriage Act, only marriages in Anglican parish churches (or by Quaker or Jewish rites) were valid, so the majority of the Huguenot registers do not record marriages after that date. Some couples, however, seem to have married in both their parish church and their own one before this Act.

Although it is customary to speak of Huguenot churches, it is perhaps more helpful to think of them as congregations, as church implies a physical building and most moved to different sites at various stages in their histories. Since it is the name of the site often given in records, this can be confusing, implying that there were more congregations than there actually were. In London, which had the largest Huguenot population, they were also amalgamated as people were assimilated into the general population and the congregations dwindled.

Often the main, or indeed the only, indication of a congregation is the inclusion of a minister in the records of the Royal Bounty, a government fund to give charitable aid to Protestant refugees, which is described in more detail in Chapter 4. This should not be taken as evidence of a sizeable community. As ministers were forcibly exiled from France but ordinary people forbidden to leave, there were possibly too many ministers to be kept fully occupied. Some of these congregations seem to have been of such short duration that it is possible that a minister was sent because a town had a few Huguenots and the church authorities wanted to create a settlement and perhaps to ensure that the people did not leave their church for the Anglicans. Several refugees from France, for example, came to the port of Falmouth in Cornwall in 1685 and they were assigned a minister. Six years later, in 1691, the minister reported that his congregation was now down to three or four people. Those who had been there had probably never intended to stay permanently.

The minister Jacques Fontaine, a nonconformist, mentions in his memoirs that there were three or four French families in Taunton to whom he acted as minister when he and his family were living there. It is possible that this was the size of many of the small and short-lived congregations mentioned below. They would not have had a separate building for worship, but would have met in the house of the minister or a member of the congregation.

London

Huguenots in London settled in three main areas: the City of London, the East, especially in and around Spitalfields, and Westminster. All the churches in the East End were nonconformist, i.e. did not conform to the Church of England's liturgy. Those in Westminster were both conformist and nonconformist. Their histories are sometimes complicated, as they closed down or amalgamated with other churches. The genealogist needs to have at least a knowledge of the changes in order to track what might have happened to their own families. There were also a number of small congregations for which no records survive in and around the metropolis.

City of London Churches

Dutch Church at Austin Friars
The first church for Dutch refugees was established in 1550 at the Church of Austin Friars. The registers have been published in two books. The first covers 1559–67 and is by A.A. van Schelven. His *Kerkeraads-protocollen der Nederduitsche vluchtellingen-kerk te London* (Church council protocols of the Dutch refugee church of London) was published in Amsterdam in 1923. It has inaccuracies and there is an annotated copy in the Guildhall Library (GL). The second consists of an alphabetical transcript by W.J.C. Moens, *The marriage, baptismal and burial registers . . . of the Dutch Reformed Church, Austin Friars* (1884). This also has errors. The original is held in LMA and there are filmed copies there and at the Society of Genealogists (SoG).

Threadneedle Street
The mother church of all the French and Walloon communities in England, this was also the main church in London in terms of its size, power and longevity. It was nonconformist. The first building burned down in the Great Fire of London in 1666 but was rebuilt. In 1840 the site was needed to construct the Royal Exchange and the congregation used the chapel of

The Dutch Church in Austin Friars

Founders Hall until 1843, while a new church was being built at St Martin Le Grand. The Post Office bought this site in 1887 to construct new premises for its operations. After short periods in temporary chapels, the church relocated to Soho Square in 1893. It is now the sole surviving French Protestant church in London. The published registers date from 1600 to 1840. Subsequent registers are with the archives in Soho Square. Services are in French with bilingual services held every month.

Jewin Street/St Martin Orgars

This conformist congregation was established in 1686 in Jewin Street, off Aldersgate. By 1692 it was meeting in Aldermanbury. In 1701 it moved to the old parish church of St Martin Orgars, off Cannon Street, where it remained until its closure in 1823. In 1689 it established another congregation in St James's Square and in 1690 it formed a pastoral and then administrative union with the Westminster congregations of St James's

The surviving French church in London, now in Soho Square

Square, Hungerford Market and Le Quarré. The registers from 1698 to 1762 survive.

East London churches

All these were nonconformist. Because they did not come under the direct authority of the Bishop of London, as the conformist churches did, they were able to appoint their own ministers, who moved between the various congregations in a bewildering manner. There were many unions and amalgamations as congregation numbers fell or ministers fell out with each other and transferred to other churches. It seems that church members were loyal to particular ministers and most moved with their favourite minister.

St Jean, Spitalfields

This church was established in 1687 in St John Street, Spitalfields. Its registers start in 1687 and end in 1823. It was united with Threadneedle Street in 1827.

La Patente, Spitalfields/Brown's Lane

This church was established by Letters Patent (hence its name) from James II in 1688 and should not be confused with the other church named La Patente in Soho. Both churches had the same ministers and regarded themselves as united but kept separate records. La Patente, Spitalfields met initially in Glovers' Hall, Beech Lane, just outside the City of London. By 1701 it had moved to Paternoster Row, south of Spitalfields Market. From 1716 to 1740 it met in Crispin Street. The next move was to Brown's Lane. In 1785, this La Patente merged with Threadneedle Street. There are registers from 1689 to 1785.

Church of the Artillery

The congregation was founded in Petticoat Lane in 1691 and moved to Artillery Row in 1695, when it took the name by which it is known. A new church (which still survives, though it is now occupied by offices) was

The Church of the Artillery in Artillery Row

opened in 1766 and in 1786 the congregation merged with that of Threadneedle Street. Registers start in 1691 and finish in 1786.

Wheeler Street
This was founded around 1700 in Three Crown Court, off Wheeler Street, sometimes given as Willow Street. In 1703 a union with the Petit Charenton in Soho was established. In 1742 the congregation left to join that of La Patente, Spitalfields. The registers cover 1704–42.

Swanfields
The congregation met in Cock Lane and then in Slaughter Street, Shoreditch. The registers cover 1721–35.

Hoxton Chapel
The chapel is first mentioned in 1714. Registers from 1751 to 1783 survive and it was closed in 1785.

Jacob Bourdillon, a minister, compiled the Répertoire Générale (General Catalogue) of baptisms from notebooks kept by the pastors of Bell Lane (1709–16), Brown's Lane (1719–40), Crispin Street (1695–1715), La Patente, Spitalfields (1689–1774) and Le Marché (five baptisms in 1709). This has also been published by the Huguenot Society. Only the entries which do not appear in the registers are given in the publication, as well as full entries for Bell Lane, Brown's Lane and Le Marché, as there are no other records for these congregations.

Westminster churches

The Savoy Church/L'Église des Grecs (The Greek Church)/Spring Gardens
The other influential French church in London was the Church of the Savoy in Westminster. It was established in 1661, although it appears that Huguenots had been living and meeting in Westminster before this date. Charles II gave the Huguenots in Covent Garden permission to use the church in the Savoy, an ancient royal palace, on condition that they conform to the Anglican Church and use the Book of Common Prayer, translated into French, in their services. A few years after 1675, this church was in such disrepair that it was closed, although the name continued to be used by its governing body. In 1682, the congregation relocated to L'Église des Grecs (the Greek Church) in Hog Lane (later renamed Crown Street, present-day Charing Cross Road). In 1709, a chapel in Spring Gardens was built. This site was abandoned in 1757, and the congregation met in the Greek Church until 1822, when they moved to Edward Street (present-day Broadwick Street in Soho). From 1845, the congregation was moved to Shaftesbury Avenue, where it became known as the French

Episcopal Church. The building here was sold in 1925, although the last baptism seems to have taken place in 1900. The earlier registers are missing. Marriages begin in 1684; baptisms start in 1703 and continue to 1822.

There was also a Dutch chapel in the Savoy, but no records have survived.

Hungerford Market/Castle Street
This conformist congregation was established in 1688. In 1691 it was united for pastoral and administrative purposes with the congregations of Le Quarré, St James's Square and Jewin Street. It moved to Castle Street off St Martin's Lane in 1701 and its congregation was absorbed by Le Quarré in 1762. Registers cover 1688–1754.

Le Quarré/Le Carré (The Square)/Berwick Street
This conformist congregation was granted the use of the chapel in Monmouth House in King's Square (present-day Soho Square) in 1690. In the same year, it became part of a pastoral union which also included St James's Square, Jewin Street and Hungerford Market. Between 1694 and 1769 it met in nearby Berwick Street. The registers cover 1690–1788.

Chapel Royal, St James's Palace
The marriage register from 1700 to 1754 and baptisms from 1738 to 1756 for this conformist congregation exist, which suggests that the first register of baptisms is missing. The last registers may also not be extant as the chapel was used until 1809, when it burned down.

St James's Square/Swallow Street, off Piccadilly
This short-lived conformist congregation was established in 1689 as an off-shoot of the Jewin Street congregation in the City of London. The congregation moved to Swallow Street, off Piccadilly, in 1694. It was united with Le Quarré in 1707 and the building closed in 1710. Registers cover 1689–1709.

Glasshouse Street/Leicester Fields
The nonconformist church of Glasshouse Street was established off Piccadilly in 1687 and moved to Leicester Fields in 1693. In 1786 the church was closed and the congregation merged with Le Quarré. The building was taken over by Congregationalists and survives today as a chapel in Orange Street, off Leicester Square. The registers cover 1688–1783.

The Tabernacle, Milk Alley
This seems to have been a separate nonconformist congregation but its volume of baptisms (1710–19) was used by Leicester Fields from 1725 and

The church of Leicester Fields, now a Congregationalist chapel.

is published by the Huguenot Society with Glasshouse Street's records (although this is not mentioned in the volume's title).

Rider Court
This small nonconformist congregation was effectively an annexe of Leicester Fields. Registers cover 1700–83 and baptisms of a particular family can be found in the registers of both.

La Patente, Soho
This nonconformist church was established by Letters Patent (hence its name) from James II in 1688 and should not be confused with the other church named La Patente in Spitalfields, although the two congregations had the same ministers and regarded themselves as united until 1719. La Patente, Soho was established in Berwick Street in 1689. In 1692 it moved to Little Chapel Street. In 1784 it was amalgamated into L'Église des Grecs. Registers cover 1689–1782.

The Four Churches
The churches of West Street, Le Petit Charenton, Crispin Street and Pearl Street are sometimes known as the Les Quatre Églises (the Four Churches)

and were conformist. They were based around Newport Market in the Covent Garden area and seem to have been very closely associated, using the same ministers.

West Street, Newport Market
Founded in 1690, the church was also known as La Tremblade, presumably after the place in Saintonge from where the first members of the congregation came. It originally met above the Market House, but moved to West Street in 1693. In 1695 it formed a union with the Crispin Street church. Its registers date from 1706 to 1743, when it merged with the Greek Church. When the congregation relocated to West Street, its old premises were taken over by a different congregation, which seems to have lasted only about six months and for which no records have been found.

Le Petit Charenton (The Little Charenton)
This very short-lived congregation, named after a famous church in Paris, was established in Newport Market in 1701 and merged with West Street in 1705. The registers for this period survive.

Crispin Street
Established in 1694 and following its merger with Pearl Street in 1701, the congregation moved to premises in Crispin Street. It may have taken over the old site of La Patente and ended up merging with La Patente in 1716.

Pearl Street
Founded in 1699, the registers end in 1701, when the congregation was absorbed into Crispin Street.

Dutch Chapel Royal
There was a chapel in the Palace of St James in Westminster. Although not formally a Huguenot church, it is possible that descendants of Dutch refugees as well as those of the Dutch Reformed Church in Westminster used this for worship, rather than travel to Austin Friars. The registers have been transcribed, but not translated from Dutch. Kretschmar, F.G.L.O., *De registers van de 'Dutch Chapel Royal' 1694–1775* (Jaarboek Central Bureau Voor Genealogie, Amsterdam, 1964). The originals are in TNA.

Other congregations in the London area for which no records have been found:

Blackfriars

This was a nonconformist congregation established by Letters Patent in 1688 and last mentioned in 1718.

26

Chelsea

There were two, apparently small, congregations in Chelsea and Little Chelsea – one conformist, the other nonconformist – which are first mentioned in 1718. The Little Chelsea meeting house was noted on a map published in 1746 but there are no other records of these congregations.

Greenwich

The Huguenots here had a conformist chapel mentioned in 1687 and still in existence in 1718. There are no extant records of it. The members of the congregation, however, seem to have had their ceremonies of baptism and marriage carried out (or perhaps repeated) in the parish church of St Alphege, presumably to provide legal proof. As there was no burial ground at their chapel, burials also took place in the parish churchyard.

Hammersmith

A conformist church was established around 1702 and is last mentioned in 1756.

L'Ancienne Patente (The Old Patent)

This nonconformist congregation was probably established in 1688 by Letters Patent, like the other churches of the same name, but it was separate from them. However, it is first mentioned only in 1699, by which time it had taken over the Berwick Street premises after La Patente, Soho moved out in 1694. It disappears around 1710.

L'Église de l'Hôpital (The Church of the Hospital)/L'Hôpital

L'Église de l'Hôpital, a conformist church, was built on the corner of Black Eagle and Grey Eagle Streets in Spitalfields as an annexe to the Threadneedle Street church, It was used between 1687 and 1743, when the congregation left to go to L'Église Neuve. The building then served as a Methodist chapel.

L'Église Neuve (The New Church)

This building, one of the oldest in East London, was built in 1743 on the corner of Church Street (now Fournier Street) and Brick Lane for the congregation from L'Église de l'Hôpital. It closed in 1809 and was taken over as a Methodist chapel, then became the Machzike Adass or

*The church,
originally
L'Église Neuve,
is now a mosque.*

Spitalfields Great Synagogue and today is the Jamme Masjid Brick Lane Great Mosque.

Marylebone Chapel

This conformist congregation is known to have existed between 1717 and 1781, but might have been established earlier.

Quaker Street

This congregation is mentioned only in 1700, and may have been established the year before. The Bishop of London, alarmed at the number of refugee churches springing up, was probably responsible for closing it down immediately.

The Pest House

In 1681 the Corporation of London granted refugees the use of a disused Pest House (previously used to isolate plague victims) near Bunhill Fields as an almshouse for the elderly and sick. In time, this developed into the French Hospital (see Chapter 4). A minister was appointed to serve there. The records have not survived but it is unlikely that there was a substantial number of baptisms or marriages there.

Wandsworth

Initially nonconformist, this congregation is first mentioned in 1573 but was later referred to as being under the jurisdiction of the Archbishop of

Only the burial ground used by the French in Wandsworth survives.

Canterbury, suggesting that it had become conformist. The community here was involved in textile dying and printing, as well as hat-making, for which they were famous. A number also made brass plates, kettles and frying pans. The Anglican parish registers contain many foreign names and it is likely that a number of the congregation, as elsewhere, had baptisms and marriages conducted in the local church, which was near their meeting house. In 1787, there is a reference to their imminent closure, with the congregation being transferred to London. In 1792 their meeting house was taken over by Methodists and was pulled down in 1882.

The congregation used a burial ground, known locally as Mount Nod, on East Hill. No written records survive. The memorial inscriptions were transcribed in 1879 and a copy placed in the Huguenot Library (HL). They were also published in the *Proceedings*. By this time, any earlier gravestones had disappeared or become illegible and most of the names are clearly English.

Wapping

A French church at Wapping on the riverside in East London was set up in 1702 primarily for Jersey and Guernsey mariners from the Channel Islands, but also used by local French inhabitants. Initially it was nonconformist, but later conformed to the Church of England. It is last mentioned in 1747.

Kent

The Strangers' or Walloon Church, Canterbury

Possibly inspired by the Huguenot settlement in Sandwich, Huguenots were invited to Canterbury in the hope that they would boost the local textile economy. In 1575 they were granted the use of the parish church of St Alphege, although they were nonconformists. They also used this church's burial ground and are entered in the parish registers. This congregation was known as the Walloon Church. About a year later, it was realised that St Alphege was too small to accommodate them and they were offered the use of Canterbury Cathedral's crypt. Registers start in 1581, the year they moved to the cathedral, and include entries of deaths. Some of the baptism entries appear in both the Walloon Church registers and those of the parish churches in which they lived. A weekly service in French is still held.

Malthouse Church, Canterbury

Around 1709, a group split off from the congregation worshipping in Canterbury Cathedral and moved into premises nearby within the cathedral's precincts. The last entry in the baptism register is in 1745 but

Weavers' houses on the River Stour in Canterbury

there is one in 1823, which was found on a loose scrap of paper. Only two marriages in 1743–4 are entered in the baptism register, which suggests that the records are not complete.

Dover

The first French church at Dover was founded in 1646; it was nonconformist. By the 1670s the congregation was almost non-existent. Another French church, this time conformist, was established in 1685, when the Huguenot church at Guisnes near Calais was demolished following the Revocation of the Edict of Nantes. Part of the congregation fled to Dover and part went to Cazand in Holland.

The Dover baptism and marriage registers cover 1647–1721 but may not be complete: the later congregation was larger than the number of ceremonies recorded suggest so it seems likely that some people used the local Anglican churches. The church had no burial ground and only deaths between 1685 and 1690 were noted. The registers were transcribed by F.A. Crisp and privately printed in 1888. The church registers of Guisnes and Cazand were published (Huguenot Society Quarto Series (HSQS) Vols. III and XXXVI). All three, plus the registers of Le Mans, have now been issued on CD-ROM by the Huguenot Society.

Rye

During 1562 a number of refugees from religious conflicts in Dieppe and Calais, just over the Channel, and later Rouen, arrived in Rye. They used the local parish church but by 1568 they had their own minister. As fresh waves of anti-Protestant incidents broke out in France, more people arrived and the authorities listed all the 'strangers' in the town. The next influx came after the St Bartholomew Massacre in 1572, but individuals arrived between these two peaks. In 1586, the town council wanted them to go – they said they could no longer support such a large number. By 1590, the community was greatly reduced and only 20–30 remained by 1622. The last mention of the congregation comes in 1728.

The members of the community here seem to have conformed to the Church of England and used the parish church, perhaps with their minister officiating. Baptisms, marriages and burials are therefore entered in the Anglican parish registers.

Sandwich

In 1550 the nonconformist Walloons here were granted the right to have their own church under their own discipline. Soon afterwards Catholic Mary I came to the throne and the congregation disappeared, presumably returning to their homelands. Under Elizabeth I, some returned but this time the congregation conformed and used the local parish church for its ceremonies. In 1561 the Crown issued a warrant to the local authorities in Sandwich to receive a group of settlers from the Strangers' Church (Austin Friars) in London. In December of that year twenty-five families arrived. A few years later, in 1568, this small Dutch community was joined by a number of Walloons, who established their own congregation. No records from their congregations survive but the names of the first settlers were listed in *Collections for the History of Sandwich* by John Boys, published between 1786 and 1792. The French-speaking group was relocated, along with some from Winchelsea, to Canterbury in 1575.

Other congregations in Kent for which no records have been found:

Boughton Malherbe

Around 1681 the Marquis de Venours bought land in Boughton Malherbe to assist his poorer countrymen and in 1682 twenty-five families from the Savoy Church relocated there. They were soon joined by another eighteen but by the end of the year the settlement was no longer in existence. The location was inconvenient and there were problems with the minister. Some people appear to have relocated to Hollingbourne, others went to

Lenham and Rainham, where they appear in the parish registers. Where the majority went is not yet known.

Faversham

This conformist congregation was established in the 1680s. The Anglican minister of the parish of Ospringe made notes of some baptisms in the French congregation in the late seventeenth century. The congregation is last mentioned in 1717. From the time of Elizabeth I gunpowder was manufactured here and the factories were owned or managed by people of Huguenot origin in the eighteenth century; at least some of their employees were French.

Maidstone

The first mention of a church in Maidstone is in 1567, when the town's authorities sought permission to invite threescore (sixty) families to settle there. To judge by the names in a list of twenty-nine inhabitants and their families born overseas, made in 1585, those who responded were all Dutch. In 1622 when another list of strangers in Maidstone was drawn up, there were then eleven households. The majority of the names appear to be English, probably because the clerk wrote down an approximation of their original names. In 1634 the former minister of the Dutch Protestant church there wrote to the government complaining that the Archbishop of Canterbury had tried to suppress him. In 1747 an Ellen Clerembauld applied for a grant from a French charity and produced a certificate attesting her baptism in a Maidstone parish church.

East Anglia

Norwich, Norfolk

Like all the earlier churches, this was nonconformist. From medieval times there were long-standing links between the merchants of the Netherlands and Norwich, the Dutch exporting cloth and other goods made in Flanders, and importing wool and skins, valuable articles at that time. Later the English began to weave and dye their own cloth, which was exported to continental Europe, including to the Netherlands and France. Some Dutch merchants lived in the town and at least one Frenchman is mentioned in records there in 1507. It was therefore a logical place for religious refugees to go after 1520, when Charles V, the (Catholic) Emperor of the Holy Roman Empire, which then ruled the Netherlands, issued decrees against Protestants. It appears that they were granted a place of worship in Norwich during the reign of Edward VI, but it is not known where. The founding of a community, however, came about for other reasons. The harsh winter of 1564–5 brought hardship to Norwich. The sheep, on which the city depended for its wool trade, died in great numbers so there was no work for the cloth trade workers. The Corporation of the city considered the advantages that skilled foreign weavers might bring and passed a resolution 'to invite divers strangers of the Low Countreys, which were now come to London and Sandwich for refuge' to move to Norwich. The ruling body of the Dutch Church of London persuaded some of those in Sandwich to relocate to Norwich, as well as to Colchester and Lynn (present-day King's Lynn). Most were Dutch speakers, but there was a small French-speaking Walloon contingent.

In 1565 Elizabeth I issued a licence in the form of Letters Patent granting power to the Mayor and Corporation of Norwich to receive thirty men in the wool trade, their families and servants: these formed the nucleus of the community there. Three years later the number had increased to at least 1,132 Dutch-speaking people, and 339 Walloons.

As the proportion of Dutch strangers was about ten times the size of the Walloons they needed a larger place to worship. The Corporation gave them the use of the choir in the church of the Black Friars, where they held their first service on 24 December 1565, and in 1713 they took over the whole building. By 1805 the size of the congregation had reduced so much that the lease the Dutch church had been granted was reassigned: the church was then to be used as a place of worship for the inhabitants of the local workhouse. Later it was used by the Primitive Methodists, who in 1886 sold the lease to a Mr Taylor and others. However, the Dutch retained the right to use it on two days, a Sunday and Monday in each year. A service in Dutch is now held yearly in the old church in the month of June by the minister of the Austin Friars church in London. The registers are in LMA.

The Bishop of Norwich gave the French-speaking Walloons, also nonconformist, the use of the Bishop's Chapel. In 1637 they moved to the church of St Mary the Less, which, after their congregation was dissolved in 1846, was taken over by a nonconformist sect called the New Jerusalemites. The registers of the Walloon church cover 1565–1832 and have been published (HSQS, Vol. I, also on CD-ROM).

Thorney, Cambridgeshire

The flat lands of East Anglia and the Low Countries on the other side of the North Sea are very similar and faced similar problems of flooding. The Dutch had long been accustomed to draining land and creating embankments. When a Dutch engineer, Sir Cornelius Vermuyden, was engaged to undertake major works in the Fenlands, he naturally recruited experienced compatriots. The Level of Hatfield Chase extends over a portion of the Isle of Axholme at the north-west corner of Lincolnshire and is partly in Yorkshire. Work to drain it began in 1626. Two years later, following increased persecution against the Huguenots in Flanders, eighty families fled and settled here, forming a nonconformist congregation. Seven years later, in 1635, there was another large influx of artisans and agriculturists, hoping to farm the newly drained land, from Normandy and the Walloon country.

It seems that a number of the refugees brought to Hatfield Chase to work decided to relocate to the Bedford Level, in the Isle of Ely at the other end of Lincolnshire on the border with Cambridgeshire, because a French church first began to assemble at Thorney in 1652 and many of the names are the same as those in the list of Sandtoft inhabitants. From this, and other documents, some fifty-three families can be identified as connected to both Levels. The Thorney settlers seem to have come largely from Guisnes as the register (HSQS, Vol. III) includes almost every name found in the Thorney register, which contains baptisms from 1654 to 1727.

Colchester, Essex

It appears that in 1551 there were sixteen to eighteen aliens with Dutch-sounding names resident in Colchester, probably businessmen. Then in 1563, following the influx of refugees from the Low Countries, the authorities in Colchester resolved to take in 'the numbre of Duche men banished for Goddes worde' and to establish a conformist church for them in the town. It was not, however, until 1570 that they received a licence from the Privy Council to carry out this resolution. In 1571, less than two months after the licence was granted, a return of 'strangers' in the town was made. There was a total of 185, of whom fifty-five were described as 'Old Strangers'; 175 were described as Dutch and four were French. (There were also four 'Scotch'. At this time, of course, Scotland was a separate kingdom). A full transcript appears in an appendix to the registers in HSQS, Vol. XII.

By 1586 a survey of the number of Dutch and other aliens in the town showed an increase to 1,293. During the Civil War, in which Colchester was taken by the Roundheads, many of the Dutch left, some to return to the Low Countries and others probably emigrated to North America. In 1724 there was a Dutch church and a French church. The latter was presumably established in the late sixteenth century, around the time of the Revocation of the Edict of Nantes, but there are no further details and no registers survive. It may have been connected to the congregation at Thorpe-le-Soken, about twelve miles away. The register (baptisms only) of the Dutch church starts in 1645 and ends in 1728; the original is held in LMA.

Thorpe-le-Soken, Essex

This village is about twelve miles from Colchester. In 1683 the Bishop of London asked a French pastor to go to Beaumont to preach in the parish church to a group of French refugees there. He went and preached but the parishioners objected because they were accustomed to hearing two services on Sunday and they resented having to sacrifice one. The refugees said it would be better to meet at Thorpe and petitioned the Bishop accordingly. Two years later, they asked to set up their own conformist chapel, instead of using the Anglican parish church in Thorpe as they had been doing. After a lot of negotiation with the minister there, the chapel was built and opened in 1688. The church had its own burial ground and the registers cover 1684–1726: they are published in HSQS, Vol. XX, also on CD-ROM.

Congregations in East Anglia for which no records have been found:

Canvey Island, Essex

Founded 1628, this is possibly another settlement where Dutch people were employed to drain land or to protect it from flooding. The last minister was appointed in 1655.

Halstead, Essex

The number of 'strangers' in Colchester grew so quickly that many could not find work. It was proposed that some of them should move to Halstead in Essex and by 1576 some forty families had relocated there. However, the townspeople of Halstead were antagonistic to the newcomers and half the families returned to Colchester. Their absence had an economic effect on the town and the authorities, supported by petitions from nearby villages, asked for their return. The Dutch established a conformist congregation, but by 1585 internal dissent led to some of them worshipping at the Anglican church. By 1589, the Dutch seem to have moved out of the town and, despite appeals for them to return, they stayed away.

Maldon, Essex

This fishing town had a brief, conformist congregation which lasted from 1686 to 1689. Some relocated to Colchester.

Ipswich, Suffolk

In 1681, the authorities in Ipswich promised help to a group of Huguenots who had visited the town to assess its potential for re-settling some of the refugees there. As the records of Threadneedle Street show, between 1681 and 1683 a number of people were given money to go to Ipswich. The conformist settlement there ran into trouble economically but the community lasted until the beginning of the eighteenth century. Some returned to London, others may have assimilated into the local population in the town or left to join the larger Huguenot congregations elsewhere.

Sandtoft, Lincolnshire

Although not strictly in East Anglia, the settlement in Sandtoft is included here as many of its inhabitants migrated to other communities in this region. Many of the indigenous inhabitants opposed the drainage of the Bedford Level in Lincolnshire and their dissatisfaction culminated in the riots of 1650, when the chapel at Sandtoft was defaced, the little village that had grown up around it demolished and the floodgates pulled out, re-submerging the area. The registers of Sandtoft Chapel are lost, but the names of eighty-eight people there were recorded by a local historian and republished in the *Proceedings*.

Soham, Cambridgeshire

A minister was appointed to this conformist congregation in 1688, but had retired by 1690.

Thetford, Norfolk

This was one of the towns that, like Norwich, brought in Dutch artisans to improve its economy. The church here was established by 1573.

Whittlesea, Isle of Ely, Cambridgeshire

This group was associated with the congregations at Sandtoft and Thorney. It is mentioned in 1648 but had merged with Thorney by 1654.

Great Yarmouth, Norfolk

A list of aliens made in 1571 lists over 100 households, mostly of Dutch origin, though some were from France. They were largely involved in the fishing business. How many were actually religious refugees and how many economic migrants is not known.

West Country

One of the major problems researching Huguenots in Devon is the impact of the bombing of the Exeter record office during the Second World War, when many documents were destroyed. All the wills, for example, have been lost, although a project to reconstruct them is underway. However, it seems that even before this the records of the two Exeter Huguenot churches had disappeared.

Bristol

The first refugees arrived from France in 1681, to escape the dragonnades. The majority came from around La Rochelle on the west coast of France. They were given the Mayor's Chapel of St Mark on College Green in the centre of the city for their worship, which was according to conformist principles. In 1720, the Corporation of the city asked for their chapel back, so the congregation raised money to build a chapel on the corner of nearby

The Mayor's Chapel of St Mark's, used by Huguenots between 1681 and 1727

Orchard Street, which opened in 1727. Numbers were already declining and they dwindled steadily until the congregation's dissolution in 1814. The building was taken over by the Plymouth Brethren and was later demolished.

The registers from 1687 to 1762 exist. Although the church did not have a burial ground, there is a register of burials, usually giving the name of the church in which individuals were interred. Some of the names in Bristol are also found in the records of the French churches at Stonehouse and Plymouth, suggesting this was also a trading community.

Plymouth, Devon

Established around 1682, the Plymouth nonconformist community was the largest in the West of England. The first registers are missing; only those from 1733 to 1807 have survived.

Stonehouse, Plymouth

This conformist congregation may have been established around 1684 but the surviving registers commence in 1692. The last entry is in 1789. This is one of the rare French churches that had its own burial ground.

Congregations in the West Country for which no records have been found:

Barnstaple, Devon

A conformist congregation was established around 1685 and last mentioned in 1705.

Bideford, Devon

A congregation was established around 1685 and dissolved around 1760. They seem, like other conformist congregations, to have used the local parish church for ceremonies as many names of French or Dutch origin appear in its registers.

Dartmouth, Devon

Established around 1685, this congregation seems to have initially been conformist, but a nonconformist minister was appointed in 1690. It was still in existence in 1748.

Exeter, Devon

There were two congregations here, one nonconformist and the other conformist. The conformists were given the use of the parish church of St Olave around 1685 and continued to use it until 1758. The nonconformist congregation existed between 1686 until after 1729 but it is not known where it met nor are there any records of it.

Names of French inhabitants have to be recovered from the Anglican parish registers and other official documents, like the Chamber Act Book of the Council. Ransom Pickard's article 'The Huguenots in Exeter' appeared in the *Transactions of the Devonshire Association for the Advancement of Science, Literature and Art*, Vol. LXVIII, (1936). It has an appendix listing all the French or apparently French names that he found in the local parish registers and in the lists of apprentices made free of the city 1622–1800. This article was followed up in a subsequent edition with some additional notes and corrigenda. However, Exeter had long-standing commercial links with France. The Merchant Adventurers of Exeter were granted a charter giving them a trading monopoly with France in 1560 and it is possible that some of those with French-sounding names in the city records were people simply living and trading there.

Beaminster, Dorset

Gershon Levieux, in the silk trade, took some Huguenots from Exeter to Beaminster, where he set up a business (and was subsequently buried). When a factory in Fulham failed in 1753, the machinery was purchased by Claude Passavant (who was born in Basle in Switzerland) of Exeter to help with employment for the Protestants there.

Glastonbury, Somerset

A Walloon conformist church was established here in 1551 and dissolved in 1554.

Salisbury, Wiltshire

A congregation was established here by 1689 and lasted until 1695.

Southern England

Southampton

Initially a nonconformist Walloon church, this congregation was established in 1567 by a group of refugees from Flanders. It conformed to the

Church of England from 1711. The initial aim of the town's authorities in offering a refuge was to establish a textile industry. The first settlers were later joined by Huguenots from Northern France and others from the Channel Islands, which both had long-standing trading links with the port. Although all spoke French, it must have been with very different accents and vocabulary and they had distinct cultural backgrounds. At the front of each of the registers is a list of those admitted to membership of the church from 1567 to 1665, by which year the congregation had dwindled dramatically. Ceremonies continued to be held there and entered in the registers until 1779. Today there is a Huguenot Memorial Garden in Town Quay Park and the French Church of St Julien's holds an annual service in French.

Winchelsea, Sussex

A congregation is mentioned in 1560 but nothing is known after 1589.

Ireland

This is not the place to examine the political relationship between Britain and Ireland over the centuries. Scots Presbyterians had been encouraged to settle there in the early years of the seventeenth century and it was hoped that Huguenots could also be used to increase Protestant influence in the largely Roman Catholic country. Their presence was expected to increase the commerce and prosperity of the region as well. A few individuals are recorded from as early as 1569. From 1662 there were schemes to settle Huguenots in Waterford, Clonmel, Carrick-on-Suir and Chapelizod in the far suburbs of Dublin, but these came to nothing. Small numbers of them did go to towns, like Carlow, Wicklow, Kilkenny, Belfast and Drogheda but the main location was Dublin. A second major settlement was in Portarlington, about forty miles (sixty-five kilometres) south-west of the capital, which was established in 1692 for the Huguenot veterans who had fought for William III in his Irish campaign.

Dublin

It was the dragonnades that triggered mass immigration from France and by 1686 there were some 650 Huguenots in Dublin, joining a small number of earlier migrants. In 1841 Edward Mangin, a Dubliner of Huguenot descent, compiled a list of Huguenot names, with anecdotes about the people, based on the memories of himself, his family and friends. As he was from a prosperous and well-connected background, it mainly describes the ruling classes. It is now in the HL and the list was published in the *Proceedings*.

41

St Patrick's

Following the Restoration of Charles II in 1660, the government was keen to encourage French Protestants to settle in Ireland. A plan to build a French church was mooted in 1660 – disputes over who was to pay and how much it would cost meant that one was never constructed. Instead, in 1665, the French were invited to use St Mary's Chapel in the Cathedral of St Patrick, and to conform to the liturgy of the Church of Ireland. They accepted and continued to meet there until 1816, by which time there was no longer a separate congregation: the Huguenots had assimilated into the general population. There are extant registers of baptisms from 1666 to 1687, marriages from 1680 to 1742 and, as St Patrick's had its own burial ground, burials 1681–1715. An annual service arranged by the Irish branch of the Huguenot Society is held in the cathedral each November.

St Mary's

Although extra galleries were built in the chapel of St Patrick's, by 1700 increases in the Huguenot population meant there was no longer room for everyone to worship there. It was decided to set up another conformist congregation on the other side of the river, near Capel Street, called the Chapel of St Mary, and to make it an annexe to St Patrick's. The first service there was held in 1701. In 1704 there was a split between the two congregations and the new Church of St Mary, also known as Mary's Abbey or 'little St Patrick', became independent. In 1716, a union between the two congregations took place. The Church of St Mary became a chapel of ease to the other, and one set of registers was kept for both churches. In 1740, St Mary's was closed and the two congregations united at St Patrick's. There are registers of baptisms 1705–42 and marriages 1705–16 (plus one in 1781) but St Mary's seems not to have had its own burial ground. The registers of the united churches start in 1716 and finish in 1818.

Peter Street

In the 1680s there was an increase of Huguenot refugees. Many did not want to conform to the Church of Ireland so they set up a separate nonconformist congregation. In 1692 they rented a room in Bride Street and bought a plot of ground near Newmarket to use as a cemetery. It was initially known by variations on its location, such as the Reformed Church near St Bride or the French Church of St Brigide. Between 1701 and 1711 a congregation met in a house in Wood Street. It has not been possible to identify this street. In 1711 money to build a new church in Peter Street was raised and the congregation was then known as Peter Street. Their registers of baptisms and burials are entitled 'L'Église Françoise de Golblac Lane' and cover 1701–31. A joint marriage register from 1702 to 1716 was kept with the Lucy Lane congregation and there is a joint burial register with entries from 1771 to 1831.

Lucy Lane

A nonconformist congregation was established in 1697 in Lucy Lane, north of the Liffey, with a burial ground in Merrion Row. In 1707 it united with Peter Street for pastoral and administrative purposes. In 1778, the building was sold to a Seceeding Presbyterian congregation. The separate registers of this congregation are not extant.

Portarlington

The French Marquis Henri Massue de Ruvigny (later created Earl of Galway) played a major role in William III's defeat of the Jacobite forces in 1690. He was created Lieutenant-General of the Armed Forces in Ireland and granted the estate of a Jacobite supporter who had fled to France. In 1692 Portarlington, a sparsely populated area on this estate, was chosen as the site of a new settlement. It is unique in the British Isles, being a town

Henri Massue de Ruvigny (1648–1720)

43

built from scratch as a place for Huguenots. The population comprised three sections: first, the pensioned-off officers and disabled veterans of King William's army; second, refugees who had gone to Switzerland, where their numbers were so great they could not be supported locally and were deliberately recruited by the scheme's organisers; and third, individuals who decided to relocate there. The first entry in the registers is 1694 and they continue to 1816, when the church was made a chapel of ease to the parish church of Lea. Later, Portarlington became a separate parish and the church is still used. As well as the church registers, a list of the veterans settled in Portarlington has been published (HSQS, Vol. XLI, also on CD-ROM).

Lisburn
The Crommelinck family originated in Flanders and left there because of the Spanish persecution of Protestants at the end of the sixteenth century. They relocated to Northern France. One branch of the family settled in St Quentin, where they were involved in the textile trade, using Dutch techniques, while another branch of the family settled in Haarlem. Louis Crommelin (as the name became in France) relocated to Amsterdam around 1685. In 1697 he came to London and was asked by the government to set up a linen business in Lisburn. He arrived with members of his extended family and some seventy workers. Here, with government support, they set up a linen business and are credited with establishing what became one of Ireland's major industries, although this may be something of an exaggeration, as there were a number of schemes across Ireland to encourage the spinning of flax and weaving of linen. There were already a few Huguenots living in the area, who seem to have used either the local church or the cathedral but they were joined by enough of their compatriots to establish their own church. The government provided help to erect a building in Castle Street. There was a major fire in 1707, which destroyed most of the town and a number of the Huguenots moved out to surrounding villages. The last minister died in 1812, by which time the congregation had been assimilated. The records are lost.

Scotland
On the death of Elizabeth I in 1603, James VI of Scotland became James I of England, and he and his successors continued to rule both countries. However, the two kingdoms were not united until the 1709 Act of Union, and Scotland still has a separate legal system. Calvinism, the fundamentalist wing of Protestantism, took root early in Scotland, where it was known as Presbyterianism. The Calvinist John Knox gained great influence in Scotland and when England tried to replace his Book of Discipline with a form of Anglicanism and to introduce a modified Book of Common

Prayer, there were riots and in 1638 the protests culminated in the signing of a covenant by people from all walks of life throughout Scotland to preserve their Kirk, as they called the Church of Scotland, to distinguish it from the Episcopal Church of Scotland. Presbyterianism remained the state religion.

Combined with what was called the 'Auld Alliance' between Scotland and France (England's traditional enemy), this meant that French Huguenots found Scotland a welcoming refuge. However, the climate and the long, dark winters must have come as a shock to those from more southern climes.

The existence of only one French church, in Edinburgh, is known. Originally the congregation met in the house of one of the Huguenots and were later offered the use of Lady Yester's Chapel, near the university. In 1687 the city's council granted the use of the college's common hall for the French minister to preach in and noted that he had been preaching 'this long tyme' in the chapel. This congregation seems to have lasted at least until 1816 but unfortunately no records of it, or of any other congregation that the migrants may have established, have yet been discovered. There was also a small settlement in nearby Leith.

In 1724, following the increase in persecution against Protestantism in France, two brothers, François and Jean Bochard, left Picardy in Northern France for London and were followed by others from the same area. In 1727 the Board of Trustees for Fisheries and Manufactories in Scotland proposed a project to improve the economy in Scotland. It included introducing cambric makers from France to improve the quality of Scottish linen. A Frenchman, Nicholas Dassauville, negotiated a contract to bring over from France ten skilled workers and their families, but while he was in France recruiting them he was arrested and imprisoned. A year later, in 1729, a party of five families did arrive, followed by Dassauville, who had come via London, where he had collected a group of Picardy men, including the Bochard brothers. A site near Calton Hill was chosen to build a workplace with accommodation (present-day Picardy Place commemorates the eastern end of the location). The women taught spinning to Scottish women in Glasgow and Edinburgh. In 1730 the men became burgesses and guild brethren of the City of Edinburgh, which gave them the right to trade on their own account.

There were, as in any new enterprise, problems and internal disagreements: François Bouchard (Jean had died shortly after his arrival in Scotland) returned to London in 1736, and was followed by others; a combative lawyer, William Dalrymple, arranged to rent part of the premises and caused trouble, though he was finally ejected in 1739. In 1743 the management of the enterprise was taken over by two Scottish merchants, who turned it into a highly successful business, but by 1762 only two of the original Picardy weavers were left. The numbers were depleted by those who had returned to London or by death; all were dead by 1776. Some of their children, however, remained in Scotland.

Channel Islands

The Channel Islands (Alderney, Jersey, Guernsey and Sark are the inhabited ones) were originally in the possession of the Dukes of Normandy and came under the English crown with William the Conqueror. Their laws are still based on French law and until comparatively recently the inhabitants spoke a French patois. Because the inhabitants spoke a variation of French, Huguenot refugees did not need to establish separate churches.

Sark was uninhabited until 1563, when the Seigneur of St Ouen in Jersey moved there with his family and followers to prevent it being taken over by the French. A group of Huguenots moved there in 1570.

In 1750 a list of 185 French Protestants who had left France (for their religion) to live in Jersey was compiled and a copy is held in the HL. It gives names, the profession of the head of the household and the ages of everyone included. The majority of them were from Normandy, which is very close to the Channel Islands. The list is supplemented by the town or village of origin of some of those included, as well as further details of their experiences in France. Details of a few for whom Jersey was a staging post on the way to England are also given, as well as those who returned to France. These notes are written in French and need a working knowledge of the language.

Chapter 3

RESEARCH PLAN

Starting Research

For many people the only starting point is a family story of Huguenot ancestry. There is usually some nugget of truth in these stories but over the years it has often become distorted. In some cases a woman of Huguenot ancestry married into an English family and her name was lost, although not the memory of her origins. It is therefore necessary to research both the male and female lines. In other cases, there is French ancestry, but the migrants did not leave because of religious persecution.

Ideally, family historians need to trace their ancestry back to at least the mid-eighteenth century before they can begin to investigate Huguenot ancestry. By this time no religious refugees were arriving from France. It is also the point at which many family historians find themselves running into a brick wall and is therefore probably a good point at which to consider possible Huguenot ancestry. Family historians who have reached back to the sixteenth century may start to suspect Dutch, Walloon or French migration for reasons of religious persecution. This particular wave had ceased by the early seventeenth century but many Dutch people later came to Britain either recruited for specific purposes, like the draining of the Fens, or following the accession of William III in 1688.

Assimilation

Many people researching their ancestry reach a dead end in the eighteenth century. This was a time of great mobility so an ancestor who suddenly pops up might have come from a variety of places and ethnic backgrounds. If your ancestors were living close to Huguenot settlements, especially if the French churches had closed by then, you can start to check Huguenot records.

Huguenots assimilated into the general population at different times. The better-off were the fastest to join mainstream British society: they needed to form business and social links with indigenous people. Being part of the established church also gave them contacts with the important members of their local society. Membership of the Anglican Church was also essential for the ambitious up until the mid-nineteenth century, because those who wished to attend the only English universities (Oxford and Cambridge) or to practise a number of professions had to swear an oath to uphold the Anglican Church. Like Quakers, strict Huguenots did not swear oaths and this, combined with nonconformist Calvinist beliefs, would have impeded their career progress.

The wealthy also tended to move out of crowded, noisy, smelly cities and town centres to the suburbs, although they would have maintained business premises at the centre of trade. In the suburbs there would be no Huguenot community, which accelerated the process of assimilation.

The poor tended to remain longer within their communities because their common ancestry was a source of support and financial assistance. Sharing Huguenot descent also gave poor people a sense of difference from those around them, a mark of individuality and being in some way special that perhaps went some way to compensate for their hardships.

The main clues to Huguenot ancestry are:

- Names
- Locations
- Occupations

Names

A forebear may have consulted a dictionary of British surnames and found that their name had a French origin and therefore assumed that it meant French ancestry. However, most surnames of this type predate Huguenot immigration. This is because, with the accession of William the Conqueror in 1066, Norman French became the legal language of government. When surnames first began to be used in the Middle Ages, many people were described with French words – Fletcher, for example, comes from *flecheur*, meaning an arrow-maker. This French origin of many surnames causes some confusion, leading to an erroneous story of ancestry being passed down.

Surnames

It should be noted that there is no such thing as a specifically Huguenot name, despite the lists that appear in articles and on the internet. Names in these lists are usually just those found in French church registers and some of them are of British people who married into Huguenot families, who had exactly the same surnames as the rest of the French population. Nor can it be assumed that all those of the same name were of the same family. There are a number of people named Prevost (meaning 'bishop') in the records of the French churches. Most seem to originate from Picardy but there are others from Poitou, places very far apart in France, so they are unlikely to be two branches of the same family. In the nineteenth century Louis Prevost became keeper of prints at the British Library – but he had been born in France in 1796, many years after the Huguenot exodus and was therefore not connected in any way to the earlier immigrants.

It is perfectly possible for both Protestant and Catholic families to share the same name, especially when it is a common one. Langlois ('English') appears frequently in Huguenot records in London but there was also a French furniture maker, Pierre Langlois, who came to England from France in the 1760s. To have worked in France he would have been a Catholic and, as he returned to Paris, he must have kept his faith. In Salem, Massachusetts, one of those caught up in the infamous witch hunts was Philip English (originally Phillipe Langlois) from the French-speaking Channel Islands.

Migrant ancestry seems obvious if an ancestor has a clearly French or Dutch name. In the past, however, a far greater number of educated people spoke French than do today – it was regarded as an accomplishment. This means that many names were simply translated – either by English clerks as individuals assimilated, or by the families themselves to escape preju-dice – particularly when the English and the French were at war, a fairly frequent occurrence. In the late eighteenth and early nineteenth century, during the Napoleonic wars, there was a great fear of French spies and potential saboteurs, which led a number of people with Huguenot ancestry to change their names. Samuel Wood and his sister Susannah, for example, entered the French Hospital in 1873 and 1877 respectively. They were descended from Francis and Catherine Dubois and the family had changed their name because of prejudice during the Napoleonic Wars. Why others changed their name is not always known. One of the people granted administration of the will of Elie Berthon proved in 1753 was James John Renault, 'known as Horatio Herdman'. How and why he came by this soubriquet is not given – perhaps he took over a business which continued to be called by the name of its previous owner and which attached itself to Renault. Such a drastic change is rare – it is more common to find translations. Other simple translations are 'Shoulder' for De L'Epaule or 'Jolly' for L'Heureux, for example.

The ancestors of the illustrator Hablot Knight Brown (1815–82), known as 'Phiz' and famous for his illustrations of Charles Dickens's work, were Huguenots originally called Bruneau. They may have chosen to change their names to fit in or they may simply have got tired of correcting clerks. English clerks often wrote phonetically what they thought they had heard, since so many people were illiterate. Du Quesne became Du Cane; Chataigne or Chatelain was written by English clerks as Shatteau or Shatting, which, understandably, became Chatting.

Dutch and English share common roots. Veld, for example is the Dutch for Field and it is easy to imagine an English clerk assuming the Dutchman

The Christening Party of Paul Dombey, from Dombey and Son, *illustration by 'Phiz'*

Mr Dombey at home, from Dombey and Son, *illustration by 'Phiz'*

before him (and who had a strong accent) had a cold. In the days when spelling was not as fixed as it is today, names like the Dutch Krocket could simply be written as the English-sounding Crockett, with nothing to distinguish its origin. The Dutch Everaert easily elides into Everett or Everard and for some names, like Boone, there is nothing to indicate that it was the name of a Dutch family. Originally the final 'e' would have been sounded and would have been dropped or become a final 'y' as the family moved into the English community, either as Boon or Bonny.

Christian names

Although surnames are not always a reliable guide, the choice of first names may indicate Huguenot ancestry. Like nonconformists in England, Huguenots had a liking for Old Testament names, such as Abraham, Benjamin, Daniel, Isaac, Josué (Joshua) or Elie (Eli). This practice was less common for daughters, but Esther, Rachel and Judith were often used. The name Magdelene, variously spelt, was also popular for women, in reference to Mary Magdelene. The use of such names deliberately proclaimed their parents' faith, because the naming practices of Catholic families concentrated on the New rather than the Old Testament and on saints.

Given the persecutions that Louis XIV and XV visited on the Huguenots, that name would rarely be chosen for their sons. Nor did they often give their children the kind of double-barrelled saints' names, like Marie-Joseph or Jean-Baptiste so often found in Catholic France. If an ancestor arrived with such a name, it is likely he or she was a first-generation convert to Protestantism.

Titles

Some titles are inherited differently in Britain compared to France. In Britain, titles descend through individuals and are attached to a person. In France before the French Revolution, some titles were attached to land. An English baron may own no property, live in a rented hovel and still be a baron, but in France if the land was lost, the individual also lost the title. Those who carried out certain municipal offices might also be given a title, sometimes called the cloche (church bell) nobility, because every town had one. These titles went with the job and were usually not heritable. The English have always loved a lord, so many Huguenots whose land or titles were confiscated continued to use them in order to give themselves status in their new country.

The word 'de' (meaning 'of' or 'from') is frequently assumed to indicate French nobility, especially if it is followed by a place name. Often, however, it is just part of the surname: Delamotte, for example, or De La Perelle. There are further problems – some families came to England via the Netherlands. For example, Andrew D'Averdine, or Andreas de Vurdun, was naturalised in 1709. He made his mark rather than sign his name so there is no clue to his preference. The English clerk translated Andreas, which suggests he may have come from the Netherlands, into Andrew. De Verdun may have been his family's original name, which had been written phonetically as D'Averdine by Dutch clerks during the family's stay there.

To confuse matters even more, a number of English people added 'de' to their names to make them sound both more fashionably French and more aristocratic. The novelist Daniel Defoe's family, for example, were originally simply Foe.

French orthography and pronunciation

As mentioned previously, spelling was not at this time fixed. Family names might be spelt differently by different clerks. This was especially a problem in the larger churches where individuals would not be as well known to the clerks as they were in smaller congregations. Regional accents in France add to the problems. At that time, there were strong differences between the French spoken in the north and the south of the country, much as there is today in England. Connected to this is a bigger problem: many French names, although written differently, would have sounded much the same. Final consonants are not usually sounded, unless followed by an 'e'. Auber and Aubert sound the same. As there is no 'th' sound in French, Arthaud and Artaud are identical, though they appear very different to English speakers. Clerks might well confuse two families with similar sounding names, especially if they did not know them well. Jumeau and Junaut would have sounded very similar. An accent over a letter is often an indication of the omission of the letter 's', e.g. Prevôt/Prevost. It is very useful to have at least a nodding acquaintance with French and to read names out loud to sort out this kind of potential confusion.

French clerks had as many problems writing down English names as their opposite numbers had with French. It takes a moment's thought or some work with a map to identify some of the addresses given in registers. Anchor Street in Bethnal Green, for example, is recorded as the recognisable Anker Street but also Encrestret, which takes some thought and a knowledge of the area. 'Langakre' is Long Acre in Covent Garden.

Locations

Besides names, the place where ancestors were living may give a clue to Huguenot origins. As they were drawn into the local communities, their own French churches closed and some started to attend the Anglican churches. Other families, however, remained nonconformist, so local records of the various non-Anglican denominations should also be investigated as different branches of the family might have taken different routes.

Christchurch,
Spitalfields

In the East End of London, the ancient parishes of St Dunstan, Stepney and St Leonard, Shoreditch had many inhabitants of Huguenot descent. The parishes of Christchurch, Spitalfields (1729) and St Matthew, Bethnal Green (1746) were created within St Dunstan as the population of Spitalfields expanded. The registers and some other parish records are in LMA with digitised copies of the original registers on www.ancestry.co.uk. Docklands Ancestor Ltd has produced a number of CD-ROMs containing transcriptions of parish registers in the East End, which are searchable by keyword.

Other parish records are held in Tower Hamlets Local Studies Library

The font in Christchurch, Spitalfields where many people of Huguenot descent were baptised

and Hackney Archives. Like most local studies libraries, they hold many deeds relating to land ownership or rental and local organisations. Tower Hamlets has, for example, a register for a local friendly society, associations whose members clubbed together to provide financial assistance to each other in times of unemployment or illness. There is also an index to burials in Bethnal Green Protestant Dissenters' Burying Ground, Gibraltar Row, next to a Congregational chapel, in use from 1792 until 1855. Some people of Huguenot ancestry were buried here. The original register is in TNA and online.

Between 1984 and 1986 the crypt of Christchurch, Spitalfields was excavated. Those with ancestors of Huguenot origin buried there may find details about them in the three works published about the project. As well as producing scientific data from the skeletons and how the individuals were buried, the researchers added information from other sources to gain more information about their background. They used Post Office directo-

The stairs to the crypt

ries, for example, to find that Charlotte Megnin, the widow of Peter, a grocer and victualler, carried on business as the landlady of the Three Jolly Weavers at 60 Wheeler Street after he died and was interred in the vault in 1839.

In Westminster, many Huguenots lived in the parishes of St Anne, Soho and St James, Piccadilly. The registers and other parish records are held in the City of Westminster Archives Centre. Parish records relating to those who lived in the parish of St Giles in the Fields, next to St Anne (where there were also substantial numbers of Huguenots), are in LMA.

In Canterbury, where there are fourteen parishes, many of the Huguenots lived in the parishes of St Alphege, St Mary Northgate, St Peter St Mildred and Holy Cross. Parish and other records here are divided between the Centre for Kentish Studies in Maidstone and the archives of Canterbury Cathedral. Some of the Anglican Church registers in

Canterbury have been published: copies can be found in the HL, Society of Genealogists (SoG) and other libraries.

In Norwich the refugee families clustered in the parishes of St Michael at Plea and St Gregory, although the lay subsidies (taxes collected in medieval times) show that they were found all over what was a comparatively small city. There may be others in the original records whose names appear British.

In Bristol, there were a number of seafarers (although the majority were weavers) so maritime records in both the local record offices (RO) and TNA should be pursued. The better-off members of the Huguenot community here started to attend St Stephens, the most fashionable Anglican parish church in the city. The poor are to be found mainly in the parish of SS Philip and Jacob. The records of both are in the Bristol RO. The families who moved away from the city centre into the countryside may be found in the Gloucestershire RO. The Bristol and Avon Family History Society have published on CD-ROM baptisms, marriages and burials of the whole Anglican diocese as well as nonconformist churches in and around Bristol.

Occupations

As mentioned earlier, the majority of Huguenots who emigrated were artisans of some description, earning their living through their manual skills. France set the fashions for the whole of Europe so the French had a head start in attracting customers to decorate and embellish both their homes and their persons. Some Huguenots were called in to set up or advise businesses but they often did not continue to employ their compatriots beyond the initial phase.

In Westminster, the craftsmen worked mainly in luxury goods. They needed to be near the Court at St James because their wares were aimed at the rich. Some were also found in the City of London, catering to the needs and desires of wealthy City businessmen, but the restrictions imposed on aliens by the City authorities meant that many could not work within the Square Mile.

Of course none of the following occupations was exclusive to Huguenots or Dutch immigrants but they did attract a high number of foreign-born workers, especially the French. Nor were they limited to these jobs: people of French and Dutch origin can be found across the whole range of skilled workers.

Textiles

By far the largest employer of Dutch and Huguenot workers was the textile industry. From the very earliest days of asylum seekers, they had been weaving fabrics: initially wool in towns like Norwich and Canterbury but later silk. Spitalfields in London's East End became a centre of silk-

Weavers' houses in Spitalfields. Note the attics, where the weavers worked to take advantage of the light.

weaving, employing many people. Extracts relating to French or Dutch families, from the records of apprenticeships to members of the Weavers' Company, to which many Huguenots belonged, have been published (HSQS, Vol. XXXIII).

The Courtauld family, now best known for textiles, came to the silk-weaving business late. They were initially metalworkers. It was George Courtauld (1761–1823) who established a textile business in Pebmarsh, Essex. His son, Samuel, expanded the business and created a highly successful family firm. Some of the profits they made went into founding the Courtauld Institute of Art in London, restoring Eltham Palace in south London and many other philanthropic and artistic causes.

A more typical family history is found in the Lekeux family, descended from Anthoine Le Keux (or Le Queux), a Walloon who had come to Canterbury via Sandwich in the late sixteenth century. The family became well established there: Philippe Le Keux was a (somewhat controversial) pastor, elected in 1646, and others were deacons and elders of the church. Peter Lekeux (1648–1723), master weaver, served his apprenticeship in Canterbury and moved to London, where he joined the Weavers' Company and married well. His bride Marie Marescaux was the daughter of one of the leading silk-weavers in the capital and he had astutely moved at a time when the London industry was rapidly expanding. His father-in-law was a wealthy man and the couple inherited property and money on his death in 1710. Peter came to play a leading role in the Weavers' Company, as well as in civil society: he became an officer in the Trained Bands (the equivalent of the Territorial Army in London), a JP, commissioner of sewers and commissioner for land tax in Middlesex, all highly important posts. His will mentions four sons, John, Daniel, William and Charles (who predeceased him), and he left substantial properties to them and his grandchildren. None followed him into the textile business: they used their inherited wealth to become merchants and 'gentlemen'.

His nephew, another Peter (1684–1743), did become a weaver and also played an important role in the Weavers' Company, as did his son, Peter III (1716–68), who was a master weaver, living and working in Spitalfields.

Engraving by John Le Keux of the crypt of Canterbury Cathedral, where his Walloon ancestors worshipped

Peter III had no children and with him the connection with silk-weaving ended. His estate was divided between other family members, not in the business and now living in the fashionable suburbs. It would be a mistake to think that the wealth of these 'master weavers' was created by a single person, working alone. They probably did very little of the actual work but gained their money by selling the silk that those they employed wove. They also married into English families, increasing their contacts with influential members of the mainstream society.

The members of the Le Keux family who remained in Canterbury also moved away from their original trade. By the nineteenth century, John Le Keux (1783–1846) had become a skilled engraver.

Not all silk-weavers, however, were Huguenots. Although it is some-times claimed that the silk industry in Macclesfield, Derbyshire, was established by Huguenots, this is erroneous, so those with silk-working ancestors in Macclesfield are virtually certain not to have Huguenot ancestry. In Greenwich, Kent, James I established a silk manufactory which employed a man from Picardy to oversee the establishment of a mulberry orchard on which silkworms could be reared. Later in nearby Lewisham a silk mill was established in 1824 on the site of a factory making guns but, again, there seems to have been no Huguenot involvement so it cannot be assumed that a silk-weaving ancestor outside London must automatically have been a Huguenot.

Metalworkers

There are a number of goldsmiths of Huguenot background. The Courtauld family, now best known for fabrics, were initially goldsmiths. Augustine Courtauld (1686–1751), was brought to England by his father in 1688. Augustine and his half-brother Peter, who was born in Soho, were both apprenticed to Simon Pontin, or Pontaine, who was apparently of French origin. Augustine's son Samuel (d. 1765), Samuel's widow, born Louisa Perina Onger, and Samuel the younger (1752–1821), son of Samuel, continued the family tradition. The younger Samuel, however, seems not to have been apprenticed or indeed done much metalwork: he just helped his mother run her business. He emigrated to America, where he became a merchant. Augustine also took at least two apprentices of Huguenot origin: Isaac Ribouleau began his apprenticeship in 1716, and Louis Ouvry was apprenticed to Courtauld in 1730. Later generations moved into the textile trade.

It was, however, as silversmiths that many made a significant contribu-tion. Paul de Lamerie (1688–1751), who worked with both gold and silver, is generally recognised as the best in his field. He was born in 's-Hertogenbosch in the Netherlands. His father, Paul Souchay de la Merie, left France in 1685 and came to England as an officer in William III's army in 1689. De Lamerie was apprenticed to another Huguenot silversmith,

Pierre Platel (*c.* 1664–1719), who was from Lille. Others silversmiths of Huguenot origin include Paul Crespin (1694–1770), Pierre Harache the younger (fl. 1698–1705), Nicolas Spimont (fl. 1742–54) and two called Peter Archambo, father and son, (1696–1767 and 1725–68).

Furniture makers
Before 1660, English furniture tended to be relatively simple and utilitarian. Chairs were not stuffed and padded – extra comfort came from separate cushions. Charles II's return from exile and his restoration to the throne in 1660 brought a fashion for luxurious furniture, which he had encountered in France. A new profession, that of the upholsterer, was introduced to England and initially a number of these were French Huguenots.

In 1953 *London Furniture Makers 1660–1840* was published. The compiler, Sir Ambrose Heal, gives names, addresses and the sources of his information, allowing more research to be pursued. The work is not confined to Huguenots and their descendants, but many are included. It was republished in 1988 and copies can be found in many libraries.

Little as yet is known about many of these craftsmen and women: names

Sir Joseph Bazalgette's memorial on the Embankment in London

which appear to be of French origin appear in the account books of the wealthy who purchased goods from them: Casbert, Lapiere, Le Sage, Pelletier, Parisels, Poitevin. Some may have been of Huguenot origin and family historians may well be able to add to knowledge of Huguenot contribution to the history of British furniture-making.

Science and technology

Sir Joseph Bazalgette (1819–91) built the London sewerage system. John Dolland was a silk-weaver who developed an interest in optics in his spare time. His son Peter set up a small optical business, which his father joined in 1752. In 1768 John Dolland became optician to George III. The business they founded was united in 1927 with the firm of Aitchison & Co. to form Dolland & Aitchison (which was incorporated into Boots in 2009).

A number were medical practitioners. Theodore Turquet de Mayerne (1573–1655) was born to a French Protestant family in Geneva and came to England in 1611 after the assassination of Henri IV of France. He became one of the doctors attending James I and his son Charles I and was knighted for his services. William Chamberlen, who fled France in 1569, settled in Southampton and founded a dynasty of surgeons. The family invented obstetric forceps. Another doctor, Denis Papin (1647–1712?), was the first to describe (and may have invented) a pressure cooker with a safety valve, which was used to prepare food that invalids would find easy to eat.

Abraham Chovet (1704–90), a pioneering anatomy lecturer, was the son

A familiar sight on many high streets, the firm of Dolland & Aitchison had its origins in the Huguenot John Dolland's interest in optics.

of a Huguenot wine merchant in London and apprenticed to Peter Lamarque of the Company of Barber-Surgeons. On completion of his apprenticeship, he briefly went to France before returning to London, where he was appointed demonstrator to the Company of Barber-Surgeons in 1734. He spent time in Barbados and Jamaica before moving to America around 1774, where he taught anatomy in Philadelphia and created a museum of anatomical specimens and models.

Horticulture
The Dutch brought their love of flower-growing, especially from bulbs, to England. A number of Huguenots and their descendants designed gardens for the wealthy. Many combined architecture and garden design, delivering a complete service for those wishing to improve their estates.

Isaac de Caus, or Caux, (1589/90–1648) was born in Dieppe. By the early 1620s he had come to England. He and a relative, Salomon de Caus, both specialised in water features and grottoes, then highly fashionable. Isaac created a grotto in the basement of the Banqueting House in Whitehall and is credited with the elaborate and celebrated grotto at Wilton House, Wiltshire, the estate of the fourth earl of Pembroke. He worked with Inigo Jones at the Banqueting House and on the development of Covent Garden.

Daniel Marot (1661–1752) was born in Paris. His father, a Protestant, was an architect and his mother was the daughter of a Dutch cabinet maker. Both father and son combined architecture with engraving and worked on various books about French architecture. Daniel left France when the persecutions that led up to the Revocation began and went to the Netherlands to stay with relatives of his mother. Here his work as an engraver, garden designer and interior designer came to the notice of William of Orange and his wife Mary, the future king and queen of England. When they came to London in 1688, Marot followed them. Here he worked for the monarchs and members of the aristocracy, like Ralph, first earl of Montagu, at Montagu House, Bloomsbury, which later became the British Museum. Marot was married to a Dutch woman, who had relatives in London, and two of their children were baptised in the Huguenot church at Leicester Fields. Later the family returned to the Netherlands.

The great map-maker John Rocque (originally Jean, c. 1709–62) was brought to England from France as a child. He started his working life with his brother Bartholomew, a landscape gardener, drawing plans and making engravings of gardens. He is now best known for his maps of London.

Paper-making
Huguenots were prominent in establishing paper-mills and introducing techniques which improved the quality of English paper. Good quality paper had been imported from France or the Netherlands, Germany and

Italy. There were some papermills in the Southampton area, set up by and employing Huguenots. Henri Portal (?–1747), who came from Poitiers to South Stoneham in Hampshire, acquired a mill in 1718. He later won the contract to make the paper for Bank of England notes, primarily because he knew how to make watermarks, then not known in England. The contract survives today, although Portal's business is now part of De La Rue, the world's largest commercial security printer and papermaker. This company in nearby Overton produces currencies, passports, security documents and the like for over 150 nations.

The professions
Not all refugees were destitute. It is surprising how many Huguenots managed to escape with their wealth. They contributed significantly to the prosperity of the City of London: the Bank of England was founded using the subscriptions of a number of Huguenots, such as Robert Caillié, Jacques du Fay, Louis Gervaise, Pierre Renau and Étienne Seignoret. The latter was fined for trading with France when England was at war with his homeland. It is clear that many Huguenots remained in touch with their old business associates. Over the eighteenth century a rather more pragmatic attitude to Huguenots in France developed, largely because of their economic importance.

The richer Huguenots' children looked to enter the professions: trade was rather snobbishly seen as an inferior occupation. The son of Jean de Blanquière, an anglicised John (1675–1753), was a politician, whose background was useful when he served in the legation in France. He became MP for several English and Irish constituencies, was a privy councillor and was ennobled as the first Baron Blanquiere.

Descendants of the Bosanquet family, originally from the Cévennes, illustrate well how generations of Huguenots contributed to English society. David Bosanquet (1661–1732) was a director of London Assurance, an early insurance company, and other members of the family also worked in insurance. Charles Bosanquet (1769–1850) was a merchant and writer on economic subjects; James Whatman Bosanquet (1804–77) was a banker and biblical historian and Samuel Bosanquet (1800–82) was a judge and also wrote on ancient history. Bernard Bosanquet (1877–1936) made a very different contribution: he was a cricketer who invented the googly. And in the twentieth century Reginald Bosanquet (1932–84) was a popular television newsreader.

A number were ministers and theologians, some within nonconformity, while others entered the Anglican Church as clergymen. Many left descendants who also entered the Church. In Ireland, where the Protestant community was smaller than in England, five first-generation migrants rose to become deans: Peter Drelincourt (1644–1722) of Armagh, Jacques Abbadie (1654?–1727) of Killaloe, his contemporary John Icard of Achonry,

Peter Maturin (*c.* 1670–1741) of Killala and Louis Saurin of Ardagh. Abbadie and Saurin had spent time in the Church of the Savoy in London before moving to Ireland.

The careers of migrant ministers in England was less impressive, but they were in competition with many more candidates. Pierre (Peter) Allix (1641–1717) was the son of Pierre Allix, pastor of the Reformed church at Alençon in Normandy. He was educated at the Protestant academy at Saumur. On graduation he became a pastor at Rouen, where he gained a reputation both for learning and preaching, which led to him becoming pastor of the main Huguenot church, Le Charenton, near Paris. Here he corresponded with other scholars in Europe and published well-received theological works. On the Revocation in 1685 he fled to England, where he founded the Huguenot community in Jewin Street, London, which later moved to St Martin Orgars and attracted many of the better-off Huguenot families. Through his theological works, he made contacts outside the Huguenot community, becoming treasurer of Salisbury Cathedral in 1690. His son John Peter (d. 1758) became a royal chaplain and successively dean of the cathedrals of Gloucester and Ely. A second son, William (1688/9–1769), became a naval commissioner, and a third, Gilbert, (d. 1767?) was a London merchant. One daughter, Marie, married Admiral Sir Charles Wager and another, Margaret, married a merchant.

Jean Dubourdieu (*c.* 1643–1720?) was born at Bergerac in south-western France, the son of a Protestant minister. Jean was educated at a Protestant seminary, which was closed in 1665 and he moved on to Geneva to complete his religious studies. After ordination he returned to France, where he was minister in various places. His father was barred from his ministry in 1680. Jean came to London on the Revocation and became a minister at the conformist French Church of the Savoy, which meant he was a Church of England minister. He had three sons, two of whom became Anglican clergymen: Peter at Kirby Misperton, Yorkshire, and Armand at Sawbridgeworth, Hertfordshire.

Sources

There is no single strategy to establish Huguenot or Dutch descent because the migrants arrived at different times and settled in different communities. The sources listed in Chapter 4 should all be consulted but first it is best to see what work has already been done. There is a great deal of family history information on the internet, but the sources of it should always be checked. There is always the possibility of error, as well as supposition presented as fact, especially if the person posting the information is not an experienced or professional researcher. However, not everything is there, so at some stage you will need to look at documents, either on film, microfiche or the originals in record offices and libraries.

Pedigrees

Henry Wagner was a nineteenth-century genealogist who had a particular interest in Huguenots and he reconstructed the pedigrees of a number of families, usually with the help of contemporary descendants. These have been listed in issue 2 of *Huguenot Families*, a publication of the Huguenot Society (see below). The files in the HL include Wagner's correspondence with people whose information he used in creating the family trees, and miscellaneous other sources, like newspaper cuttings.

As well as the Wagner pedigrees, the HL also holds a number of pedigrees that have been deposited there. Some, mainly of wealthy or titled families, are printed but others are of those that ordinary family historians have researched and typed up, or even written by hand. The names are listed in HSQS, Vol. X. These need, however, to be treated with caution. Wagner was meticulous in checking the information he received but in Victorian times, the idea of Huguenots as the admirable epitome of the Protestant work ethic led many people to claim such ancestry. Victorians were also snobbish about aristocratic descent. Genealogists of the period might either have made assumptions of links where the evidence was sketchy or non-existent in order to please a paying client. They might also not have had access to documents and other sources that are now more

Heading of an illustrated and printed pedigree from the Huguenot Library's collection

readily available. Today it is relatively easy to find out where family papers have been deposited through the National Register of Archives website, which contains the catalogues of county record offices all over England and Wales. Before this, it was not always so simple to locate where a family's archives might have wound up. Descendants might have moved a long way from the family's original home, or someone might have deposited their papers in a university library if they had some connection with a college.

Over the years, a number of people have written to the HS enquiring about possible Huguenot ancestry and research files dating from the 1960s are held in the library. The names were listed in issue 4 of *Huguenot Families* but they have since been added to.

Publications

There is a master index to the *Proceedings* of the Huguenot Society Volumes I–XXVI (1886–1997), which consists of single words, such as family names or places. At various times other indexes by subject have also been published.

There are full runs of the *Proceedings* in the Huguenot Library, in the Society of Genealogists and in other libraries. Fellows of the Huguenot Society have access to all the *Proceedings* which have been digitised and put online in the members' area of the Society's website.

Another publication of the Huguenot Society, which contains less scholarly articles, with an emphasis on individual families, is *Huguenot Families*. It has now ceased publication but all twenty issues have been put on to a single CD-ROM, published by the HS.

Records deposited with the Huguenot Library

Over the years, miscellaneous records, family papers, transcripts of material and indexes have been deposited with the Huguenot Library, which is housed by University College London with its Special Collections. The library's catalogue is online. This contains everything in the library: published books, unpublished theses, publications from overseas societies, etc. When searching the catalogue, you need to prefix keywords, authors, etc. with 'Huguenot', e.g. if you are looking for the Ferry family, you need to put 'Huguenot Ferry' in the search box. You will find this produces two publications. If you just put Ferry in the search box, you will get every book on ferries or by people called Ferry in all the University College libraries – over 350 in this case.

The library's holdings have been catalogued with details of what they contain, although not every name that appears in the originals is included. These have been published in two HSQS publications: *Huguenot*

Manuscripts: a descriptive catalogue of the remaining manuscripts in the Huguenot Library (Vol. LVI), and *Huguenot Archives*: a further catalogue of material held in the Huguenot Library (Vol. LXI). These two books repay careful study: there are many collections of documents compiled by researchers over the 120 years of the Society's existence, including transcripts of material in other repositories, like the British Library and TNA. Consulting them in the HL can save time and money in travelling to these other archives.

Family histories

With the advent of personal computers and easier methods of producing books, many genealogists have published their own family histories in books or booklets. Some are available from the family directly through the internet. The Huguenot Library has a large collection, as does the Society of Genealogists. The Guild of One-Name Studies (GOONS) is an association whose members are researching particular surnames. The list of the names is on the guild's website. Family history magazines sometimes contain advertisements from individuals tracing a particular name. Getting in touch with them might save you some work, or find you a distant cousin who may be prepared to share research work with you.

Checklist

There is no one ideal way to conduct research into possible Huguenot ancestry. Some of the sources are available in different forms: published as books and on CD-ROM, digitised and put on the internet or only in manuscript form. A research trip involves a great deal of planning. If you need to travel a long (and expensive) way to the record office of the place where your ancestors lived, you need to weigh the cost of the fare and overnight accommodation against buying CD-ROMs or investigating local libraries that may have copies of the HSQS. If you need to use censuses or get copies of PCC wills, is it cheaper to pay for them online or travel to TNA, where they are available for free? (The Prerogative Court of Canterbury (PCC) was the highest probate court for proving wills in England and Wales and the British colonies.)

There is a tendency to research one individual at a time, but it is common to find that different events are recorded in different places, especially in London. Church registers may be in one repository, land deeds in another and livery company records in a third.

Think instead in terms of individual record repositories. Shuttling between county record offices, local record offices, the Huguenot Library and other specialist libraries in order to trace the events in the life of one individual is time consuming and you may find, when you start on another ancestor, that you could also have researched aspects of his or her life in one or more of these places at the same time. When planning your research, have a form for each record office, so you will know what you need to look for in each one. Record the information needed, e.g. the date of a burial of one ancestor and the marriage of another. Then note the sources to look at, in this case the registers of churches, marriages licences and banns in a likely area and wills in the archdeaconry and commissary courts. When you get there, note the archive's reference numbers (in case you need to check them again) and whether or not the information you were seeking is there. This is important: it saves wasting time if, some months later, you forget which records you have already consulted with no result. It also helps to have this information all together on a single sheet. If you just record it in your notebook, you will spend a lot of time looking through it to remind yourself which information you have already checked.

Most record offices have an online catalogue and TNA's ARCHON directory has details of the location of all repositories. The TNA's website Access to Archives (A2A) contains the catalogues of local archives in England and Wales. Consulting these before going to the repository will save time – and may suggest further avenues of research.

Research Checklist

The following table can be used as a guide and also to ensure that no potential sources are missed. Many are not specific to Huguenots or Dutch immigrants because they had to interact with their local communities.

Source of information	Location of records
Previous research on the name: • Pedigrees • Published family history books	Huguenot Library Internet Society of Genealogists
Wills • PCC wills • Commissary Court and Archdeaconry Court wills	TNA website Wagner wills Diocesan records offices Local record offices
Denizations and naturalisations	HSQS
Charities • Threadneedle Street • Coqueau Charity • Miscellaneous Huguenot charities • Royal Bounty • Maison de Charite, Spitalfields	HSQS Huguenot Library

Source of information	Location of records
Church registers: • Huguenot churches • Anglican parish registers • Nonconformist registers	HSQS County and local record offices Published transcripts Unpublished transcripts in SoG CD-ROMs
Nonconformist burial grounds	County and local record offices
Other parish records • Ratebooks • Vestry minutes • Tithe books	County and local record offices
Coroners Inquests	County record offices Newspapers and periodicals
Censuses and head counts • Before 1841 • After 1841	County and local record offices Internet and TNA
Miscellaneous local records • Quarter Sessions • Land records (deeds, taxes, etc.) • Maps	County and local record offices
Newspapers and periodicals	County and local record offices British Library Newspaper Library Internet Dr Williams's Library
Nonconformists	County and local record offices Dr Williams's Library
Occupational records • Apprenticeships • Freemen • Professional bodies, e.g. Royal College of Physicians	HL Guildhall Library City of London livery companies County and local record offices (for freemen outside London) Archives of the professional body or association.

Chapter 4

SPECIFIC SOURCES

Most immigrants initially regard their residence as temporary. They intend to return to their homelands when the conditions that triggered their exile have changed. Places of worship provide a focal point. The French and Dutch churches kept their communities united and ensured the survival of the language and culture. They also provided education for the young and care for the elderly and poor. This was partly because one of the tenets of Protestantism was self-reliance, but it was also a way of ensuring the continuation of cultural identity. At some point, however, people start to recognise that the new lives they have created will be permanent and if they want to join the wider society they must integrate. The decision to apply for citizenship comes either because migrants need to acquire the rights that native-born people automatically gain or because they have decided to stay and become full citizens.

The records created by these two opposing impulses give good coverage of Huguenots across the economic and social spectrum. The better-off needed to put themselves on a level footing with their English competitors. The poor needed help to survive and they turned to their compatriots for support.

Denizations and Naturalisations

Generally people were granted denization by Letters Patent from the Crown or another authorised body, which was a relatively quick and simple procedure, or they were naturalised by Act of Parliament, which could be a long and costly process. Denization gave people the right to live in the country and naturalisation the full rights of a citizen: to own, bequeath and inherit property, to vote (if otherwise qualified), to pay taxes at the same rate as native-born citizens, etc. In the late sixteenth century it was not entirely clear what rights aliens had and their rights, duties and privileges were clarified over the following fifty-odd years. Initially foreigners were taxed more highly than the native-born. It is clear that many Huguenots never applied for either denization or naturalisation: presumably they were from the poorer part of the community and did not consider it worthwhile.

Between 1708 and 1710 there was a temporary relaxation of the normal formalities regarding the obtaining of private naturalisation Acts in order to make it easier and cheaper to become naturalised. The conditions were that the applicants should be foreign Protestants; that they should take and subscribe to the oaths of allegiance and supremacy. The swearing and declaration had to be performed in one of the four courts at Westminster (Chancery, Queen's Bench, Common Pleas or Exchequer) in open court; or in Scotland before the Lords of Council and Session or Lords of Justiciary or Barons of the Exchequer. Alternatively, in England, the oath-taking and declaration could take place at a General Quarter Sessions of Peace held in the county where the person lived. A fee of 1s (5p) was charged for the whole procedure, but before taking the oath the individual concerned had to have taken the sacrament within three months and had to produce a certificate to this effect at the time of making the oath and declaration in court. An entry of this certificate had to be made at the court. There were other minor conditions but this is the main outline of the provisions. If your ancestor is not found in the returns of 1708–10, it is worth searching the local Quarter Sessions records, or their equivalent in the relevant county record office (CRO) to see if he or she brought a certificate to a local court. There were no Quarter Sessions in London and Middlesex: separate Sessions of the Peace were held for the Cities of London and Westminster and surviving records are in LMA.

All denization and naturalisation records (not just Huguenots) from 1509–1800 have been published by the Huguenot Society (HSQS, Vols VIII, XVIII and XXVII, also on CD-ROM). There is also a supplement to these records (HSQS, Vol. XXXV, on the same CD-ROM) because the last thirty pages (pp. 209–40) of the second volume were not indexed, so that the names of some 1,200 persons were missing. In addition, after the publication of the first work, a further list of declarations (320 people) was found in TNA (E69/86).

Returns of Strangers

Lists of foreigners were made by various towns for a number of reasons, but often because local people were objecting to their presence, as in Maidstone in 1585 and 1622 and Colchester in 1551 and 1571. In London, fear of invasion by hostile powers was a further consideration: it was thought that foreigners might be a subversive element who could be spies or aid enemies. Returns of aliens for London between 1529–1605 have been published by the Huguenot Society (HSQS, Vol. X, also on CD-ROM). These returns are supplemented by lay subsidy records and also lists of members of the Dutch Church, Austin Friars; various state papers (Domestic Series); the Lansdowne MSS in the British Library; and several printed works. These returns list all people in the sources, not just those who might be Protestant refugees. They are not, however, a complete record of all foreigners: many records are simply missing. The editor, Irene Scouloudi, noted that a number of the people described as 'denizens' in these records cannot be found in the official records granting denization.

Lay subsidies (taxes) were based on a person's wealth, in terms of moveable goods, lands or wages, and what was included varied over time. Aliens were charged at double the rate of the indigenous population, so they are easily identifiable in the surviving records. Many have been published; those related to Walloons and Dutch refugees appear in the *Proceedings* and various other HSQS publications. There were also occasional special collections of taxes, for specific purposes, such as the relief of distressed subjects in Ireland, levied in 1642. From 1662, the Hearth Tax and other taxes replaced lay subsidies. Various tax records are held in TNA, arranged by county.

Those people recorded as being from 'the dominion of the King of Spain' or 'under the obedience of the Emperor' in these earlier returns and in the denizations and naturalisations would almost certainly have been from the Low Countries. Those from Spain itself, many of whom before 1656 were Jews living illegally in England, are simply noted as 'from Spain'. Others may have been among the few Spanish Protestant converts who sought refuge in England.

Huguenot Church Records

As well as church registers (detailed in Chapter 2) the French and Dutch churches kept a number of other records of use to the family historian. Most of the records relating to the Canterbury congregation are deposited in the archives in Canterbury Cathedral. The others are generally in the Huguenot Library or the archives of the French church in Soho Square.

Actes du Consistoire (Acts of the Consistory)

The governing body of the various French and Dutch churches was known as the consistory, equivalent to the vestry of the Church of England's parish, but without of course the local government responsibilities that the Anglican parish had at the time. The Acts were the minutes of the meetings. In general they dealt with church matters, like pastors, elders and deacons; the relationship with the English government; correspondence with overseas branches of their church; internal feuds and disagreements and the like. The church also kept a strict eye on its members and the Acts recorded transgressions of the church's moral code by the laity – and occasionally by ministers. Sinners were summoned before the consistory, which might impose penalties ranging from a simple rebuke right through to excommunication.

These Acts give an insight into the power that the authorities wielded over members of the congregation. At a meeting of the Threadneedle Street church on 15 February 1685, for example, Marie Liet opposed Isaac Le Roy's banns, claiming that Le Roi had promised to marry her. Le Roi confessed that he had written asking her father for her hand. Le Roi was urged to disengage himself from his promise fairly and give Marie satisfaction for the expenses she had incurred. He refused. The consistory noted that publication of his banns would be deferred. A week later, Judith Daufin came to the consistory and asked to be freed from her engagement to Isaac Le Roy, because he had pledged himself to Marie Liet. The authorities decided that Le Roy would be cited in church next Sunday. More dramatic stories are also recorded. In 1688 on 26 August it was noted that Louise Pere, of Mans, and her sister Madelaine Pere, wife of Alexis Pillau, had signed (presumably an abjuration of their Protestant faith) in order to get out of prison. Then they were again captured as they tried to leave France. They were put back into prison 'until God in his grace enabled them to come here'. In view of what they had endured, it was resolved to admit them to the church without exacting public recognition of their 'fault'.

The Acts of the Consistory of the Threadneedle Street church for 1560–5, 1571–7 and 1679–92 have been published by the Huguenot Society (HSQS, Vols XXXVIII, XLVIII and LVIII, also on CD-ROM). No records for the first ten years seem to have survived. The first two published volumes are not translated from French and retain the original spelling, as idiosyncratic as English spelling was at that time. The index, however, has sub-headings in English, which will give non-French speakers at least an indication of why an individual was included. The third volume was translated into English.

It is clear from the Acts that the Dutch and French congregations were in contact with the Italian Protestant church and a 'coetus', a meeting of the ministers and elders of all three foreign churches, met monthly. There was also a small German contingent who were represented. The minutes of the coetus of London 1575 (in semi-modernised French) and the consistory minutes of the Italian Church of London 1570–91 (in modernised Italian) have also been published by the Huguenot Society (HSQS, Vol. LIX, also on CD-ROM). No registers of the Italian Church have yet been discovered. By the middle of the seventeenth century, only the French and Dutch churches survived. An unpublished volume of meetings held between 1720 and 1800 of the General Assembly of the French Churches of London is also in the Huguenot Library.

A catalogue of miscellaneous documents in the HL has been published in HSQS, Vol. LI. The documents themselves have not been transcribed. They include:

Acts of the Consistories

- The Savoy Church 1736–1910 (and a number of other documents relating to the church)
- Hungerford Market/Castle Street 1688–1758
- Glasshouse Street/Leicester Fields 1693–1787
- Le Quarré/Berwick Street 1691–1744
- St James's Square/Swallow Street 1689–96
- West Street 1693–1741
- The joint vestry of Hungerford Market/Castle Street and Le Quarré/Berwick Street 1726–52 relating to a bequest made by Judith de la Barre
- Thorpe-le-Soken, Essex 1684–1726
- Quarterly payments for pew rents in the church of Le Quarré, 1779–1808 and 1812–37
- Account books of contributions from members of the united churches of Le Quarré and Leicester Fields, 1786–96 and 1828–37

Archives of the church in Soho Square

A catalogue of the records held in the archives of the French church in Soho Square has been published (HSQS, Vol. L). Most of the records here are concerned with church governance and ministers. The records include:

- Conferences of proceedings with other Huguenot and Dutch churches
- The Acts of the Consistory of the Threadneedle Street church, 1560–5 and 1571–1822
- Lists of church members 1784; 1787–90; 1807–23, 1850?; 1862; 1866, c. 1875; 1884–7; 1895–1902; and 1925 to date
- Pews and seat holders 1737–51
- List of church members and pew lists of the chapels of ease (L'Église de L'Hôpital and L'Église Neuve) 1744–96
- *Témoignages* up to 1803; those up to 1789 have been published in HSQS, Vol. XXI and on CD-ROM
- Special collections, for example to repair and build the church, or for the relief of the poor; names of contributors and recipients are often included
- Church accounts, including legacies, and other gifts and bequests (names are listed in the catalogue)
- Distribution of relief to the poor 1661–1845
- Inventories of goods of members who had received money from the church and had agreed to refund it or for their goods to be sold after death
- Fines

- Miscellaneous correspondence, mainly requesting financial assistance.

Although mainly concerned with the business of the Threadneedle Street church, there are also miscellaneous documents from other French churches in the Soho Square archives. These include:

- Distribution of money to the poor by the Savoy Church jointly with Threadneedle Street 1685–6
- List of the poor in the area of Brick Lane, Brown's Lane, Wheeler Street and Le Marché in Petticoat Lane *c*. 1715
- Minutes of the consistory of La Patente, Spitalfields 1716–86 and list of members 1783–6
- Minutes of the consistory of the Church of the Artillery 1695–1762; list of members 1758–86 and seat and pew holders 1718–59; forty-six marriage licences and five *annonces*/promises to marry. There is also some miscellaneous correspondence from this church.
- Acts of the Consistory of St Jean, Spitalfields 1755–87, church members 1770–1800 and miscellaneous correspondence

As well as church business, there are registers from the French schools and a register of apprenticeships 1753–67. There are also the apprenticeship indentures of 160 boys and girls 1725–1867. Lists of these have been published in the *Proceedings* by Keith le May.

Reconnaissances, abjurations, témoignages

Many Protestants in France after the Revocation of the Edict of Nantes in 1685 were forcibly 'converted' to Catholicism and had formally to abjure this faith before they could be accepted into a congregation in the British Isles. Reconnaissance (from the French word meaning 'to recognise') was the recognition of fault by an individual who had nominally converted to Roman Catholicism in France and attended mass or taken part in some Catholic sacrament, such as baptism of children. Catholic converts also had formally to abjure their former religion. Some notes of these are found among the Acts of the Consistories, which often include more detail, like the account of Isaac Wassellart's appearance before the consistory of St Jean, Spitalfields on 30 November 1701:

> S'est presenté devant notre consistoire Isacq Vouaslard de Guize, pour recognoistre la faute qu'il avoit faitte de retourner en France après en estre sorty, et de estre servy pour cella d'un passeport ou il estoit recognu pour papist et ensuite pour n'avoir pas tesmoingné assez de Constance dans une funeste occasion ou il rencontra l'hostie.

Il en a tesmoigne une vive douleur et en a fait sa recognoissance publique en presence de cette ég. et ensuitte a demandé d'estre fait membre de cette eg. ce que luy a esté accordé. par Mr. Balguerye, Min. de cette ég. Isaac Wassellart.

(Presented himself before our consistory Isacq Vouaslard from Guize, in order to recognise the fault he committed in returning to France after leaving it, and in using a passport which said he was papist and then for not having demonstrated enough Constancy at a funeral when he took the host. He demonstrated a vivid sadness and made his public recognition of fault in the presence of this ch[urch] and then asked to be made a member of this ch[urch], which was accorded to him by Mr Balguerye, Min[inster] of this ch[urch]. Isaac Wassellart.)

It seems that Isaac Wassellart (note the way the French clerk spelled his name) returned to France for a funeral, using a passport which stated that he was a Catholic. At the ceremony in a Catholic church, he took communion. Unfortunately the notes do not say whose funeral it was: it must have been someone very important to him for him to have taken such risks, which the Consistory probably took into account – otherwise they might have excommunicated him.

Others migrants were included in the *témoignages*. *Témoignages* were attestations of faith, from the French word meaning witness or testimony. Refugees coming to England had to be able to prove that they were both true Protestants (there was a fear of spies and informers) and also that their beliefs were orthodox. They were supposed to bring a certificate from their previous congregation (and a number were able to do so) but in the upheavals that accompanied their escape many were unable to do this. These people either had to get someone, such as another member of the family, to vouch for them or they were examined by a senior member of the consistory or another suitably qualified person. People who moved from one Huguenot community to another for whatever reason also had to provide certificates. Children of members of the congregation were usually accepted on their parents' declarations, although in some cases they still seem to have been questioned about the articles of their faith.

These records are very useful in discovering migration, whether from overseas or within England, which then points the researcher in the direction of other sources. The main lists of *témoignages*, which also include some abjurations, are found in the records of the Threadneedle Street church, published by the Huguenot Society (HSQS, Vol. XXI, also on CD-ROM). They start in 1669, so earlier records must be missing. Other congregations kept their own lists. The register of the abjurations and reconnaissances of the conformist Savoy Church 1664–1702 have also been published by the

Huguenot Society (HSQS, Vol. XXII, also on CD-ROM). Despite the title that the Savoy Church used, it is the equivalent of the Threadneedle Street's *témoignages*. Also published by the Huguenot Society, in the same volumes as the individual church registers, are the abjurations, *témoignages* and reconnaissances at the Church of the Artillery; Glasshouse Street/Leicester Square; Le Quarré; Rider Court; Hungerford Market; the Four Churches, La Patente, Spitalfields and St Jean, Spitalfields.

Information about members of the Dutch Church of Austin Friars in the City of London, who would also have had to prove the authenticity and orthodoxy of their faith before acceptance, were published in 1892 as *Register of the Attestations or Certificates of Membership, Confessions of Guilt, Certificates of Marriages, Betrothals, Publications of Banns, &c, &c. Preserved in the Dutch Reformed Church, Austin Friars, London, 1568 to 1872*, edited and translated into English by J.H. Hessels. It was issued on CD-ROM by Archive Books but is no longer available to buy, although libraries may have copies or it might be available secondhand. The attestations give far more detail about individuals than is found in the French churches' records. The confessions of guilt are not abjurations, but admissions of breaches of the church's moral code, like those found in the Acts of the Consistories of the French churches described above.

Poor Relief and Charity Records

A number of charities were set up to look after the old, sick and un-employed and to educate the children. These records provide a wealth of detail for family historians.

Relief of French Protestant refugees 1681–1687

Following the almost overwhelming flood of refugees escaping the dragonnades in 1681, the English government issued instructions, in the form of Briefs sent to parishes throughout the kingdom, to raise money to help them. The response was generous and the money received was passed to the authorities of the French church at Threadneedle Street to be distributed. The records of their disbursement have been published by the Huguenot Society (HSQS, Vol. XLIX, also on CD-ROM). The records have been generally translated into English but a few phrases have been left in French. These mainly refer to grants of clothing and shoes, which were given to many – an indication of how little they had been able to take with them when they escaped.

These lists provide a wealth of detail: occupations, where some of these migrants came from, the names and relationships of family members, numbers of children, the sums of money they received, etc. Some were given money to go to other places in the British Isles, such as Ipswich, or even abroad. In 1682, for example, Jean Castel was given £2 for his passage to Pennsylvania.

French Protestant Hospital of La Providence

In 1681 the Corporation of the City of London offered the authorities of the Threadneedle Street church the use of the Pest House, a building near Bunhill Fields just outside the city walls, which was then empty. This became a source of care for sick and elderly Huguenots and was known as the French Hospital. In the early days it was sometimes also referred to as the Bunhill Hospital. The inmates called it La Providence, meaning God's protective care. The hospital was given grants by the Royal Bounty (see below) and personal grants from various monarchs. Over the centuries it was also frequently left bequests by the wealthier Huguenots, which allowed it to continue and to provide a much higher standard of care than poor people generally received.

In 1716 a plot of land at Finsbury near the Pest House became available and responses to appeals for funds were so generous that a new building was made possible, rather than the simple extension that had been envisaged. In 1718 the French Hospital was formally incorporated and directors appointed. The hospital initially cared for both the physically and the mentally ill, with an annex for the mentally afflicted that lasted until 1791.

The hospital remained in Finsbury until 1867, when it moved to a specially built site at Victoria Park in Hackney. This building was later occupied by the Cardinal Pole Roman Catholic School, a rather ironic

The French Hospital site in St Luke's, Finsbury

The French Hospital in Hackney, used as a school

transfer of occupants. During the Second World War it was bombed and the inmates briefly relocated to Horsham, Sussex. After the war all the houses in Theobald Square, near the cathedral in Rochester, Kent, were bought and converted into self-contained flats. The square was renamed La Providence in 1958. The hospital is therefore still in existence, providing housing for people in need who can prove their Huguenot ancestry.

The records of applicants and entrants to the hospital between 1718 and 1957 have been published by the Huguenot Society (HSQS, Vols LII and LIII, also on CD-ROM). No records before 1718 seem to have survived. Earlier records are in French, and have not been translated. The applicants are apparently all from London, though the earlier records do not mention addresses. These records include summaries of the applications and decisions made by the hospital authorities. Dates of entry and leaving (usually through death) of successful applicants are supplemented by references to individuals during their stay in the hospital, drawn from other records, like the minutes of directors' and administrators' meetings. These are mainly transgressions of the rules. For example, on 11 March 1748/9 Marie Adeline, who had entered the hospital on 7 January 1748/9, was noted as: 'etant revenue a l'Hopital eprise de boisson la Compagnie luy a defendu de Sortir de la maison pendant un mois' (being returned to the Hospital taken with drink, the Company forbade her to go out for a month). Then,

In Victorian times men and women had separate accommodation, which, as the furniture shows, was more luxurious than English workhouse inhabitants experienced.

on 8 April 1749, 'La nommee Adeline & Trinquand qui etoient retenus dans la maison, S' Etant bien comportés dudepuis on leur a accorde leur liberte comme auparavant' (The named Adeline and Trinquand [another transgressor] who returned to the house, conducted themselves well since then so were given their liberty as before). However, on 2 June 1750, 'La nommee Marie Adeline revenue dans la Maison eprise de boisson La Compagnie luy a deffendu de Sortir de l'Hopital pendant 3 mois d'aujourd'huy' (The named Marie Adeline having come back to the house taken with drink, the Company forbade her to go out of the Hospital for three months from today).

She was the widow of Jean Adeline, who entered in 1737 and in 1739 left the Hospital because he had contravened the rules. Marie seems to have reformed: she remained in the Hospital until her death in 1759 at the age of eighty.

The minutes and the original documents produced to support applications are stored in the Huguenot Library and occasionally contain additional information. Because the editors of the published records have arranged them alphabetically, it is a very useful tool to discover family relationships – it is common to find two, three or even more generations of the same family applying to the Hospital. People are also usually able to give details of their descent from the original refugee, which is a godsend to researchers. Even if people no longer attended the French Church, they were entitled to apply and their addresses suggest further avenues of research among Anglican parish records and local nonconformist churches.

The Coqueau Charity

Not much is known about Esther Coqueau. She was a spinster, living in the parish of Christchurch, Spitalfields and was plainly well off. When she died in 1745, she left a number of bequests, one of which required the directors of the French Hospital to pay a monthly sum of 10s (50p, at a time when the average wage was about 75p per week) to ten poor unmarried women or widows over the age of fifty until they died. When a vacancy in their number arose, it was to be filled by another woman. She left a similar sum to the French Church to found another Coqueau Charity.

Records of applicants to and beneficiaries of the Coqueau Charity, administered by the French Hospital, are included with the records of applicants to the French Hospital in the HSQS volumes.

Maison de Charité (House of Charity), Spitalfields

Many of the Huguenot refugees went to live in Spitalfields and Bethnal Green. The majority were poor and were involved in the silk trade, especially as weavers. A charity to help them was founded in the winter of 1689/90. This charity was also known as La Soupe (The Soup), since it supplied food to poor people and their families. Records were kept of how many 'portions' or allocations of food were handed out per week; age, number of children and where claimants were living is included. In 1737 a portion was composed of eight ounces of dry bread, four ounces of bread in the soup, and half a pound of meat.

The earlier records are missing and there are gaps in the surviving ones. Extant records from 1739 to 1741 have been published by the Huguenot Society (HSQS, Vol. LV, also on CD-ROM). They are in French, but since they follow a standard format they are not too difficult to understand with a dictionary.

Relief of the poor

The churches all took their responsibility towards the poor seriously. The HL holds the following records of the smaller churches:

- The Savoy Church's account books relating to money received and disbursed to the poor 1794–1901 and monthly lists of payments to the poor 1841–57
- Le Quarré's treasurers' accounts and Chapel and Poor accounts 1797–1836 and two further treasurer's account books relating to the poor 1756–90 and to general accounts between 1762 and1797. There is also an account book relating to the 'Bread Charity' from 1810 to 1836 and a fund for the relief of the poor 1813–28, as well as lists of the poor for 1830–6
- An account book of the Chapel Royal in St James's Palace detailing receipts from the poor box and payments to the poor 1738–1809
- An account book detailing monies collected and distributed to the poor of the French church in Sandwich between 1568 and 1572
- Deacons' accounts of monies received and distributed for poor relief 1631–47 in London, Rye, Sandwich and Dover

The Norwich French Church Charity

Norwich prospered until the early nineteenth century, when the invention of machinery to use steam to power looms meant that the swift rivers of the north gave that region a major advantage over the flatlands of East Anglia; the industry moved away. By 1832 the congregation of the Huguenot church was negligible, both because of the decline in the clothing industry and assimilation into the local population. The church's property was transferred to the French Hospital in London, with part of the income being reserved to apprentice poor boys of Huguenot ancestry. The church itself was sold in 1902 to establish the Norwich French Church Charity. Half the income from the invested proceeds still goes to the French Hospital, with the other half being used for the benefit of Norwich and people from Norfolk generally in terms of education and training. Priority is given to those who can prove Huguenot descent.

Royal Bounty

From 1686 the English monarchs, from James II to Queen Anne, issued Briefs, royal letters authorising the collection of money from people throughout the kingdom in order to assist Huguenot refugees. In addition there was an annual sum from the Privy Purse between 1696 and 1804; there were also some private donations. From 1804 Parliamentary grants were made until 1876, when the Royal Bounty ceased. From then on, needy Huguenots were expected to apply to the Anglican authorities for relief or to turn to their own charities.

The money was distributed by three main committees: the English, the French and the Ecclesiastical Committees. The English Committee's main role was to scrutinise the accounts produced by the other two. There were different funds for the laity and the clergy. The French Committee dealt with ordinary people, while allocations to the clergy were administered by the Ecclesiastical Committee. Between 1717 and 1730 a fourth committee distributed money to proselytes, people who had converted from Roman Catholicism to Protestantism.

In London there were two sub-committees dealing with the distribution of grants, one for West London (usually called the Department of Westminster and Soho), and the other for East London (usually called the Department of London and Spitalfields). The Bounty payments were not confined to London: money was sent by the French Committee to other settlements, including the Channel Islands.

Only the registers of the French Committee dealing with the lay people are deposited in the Huguenot Library, with the exception of four minute books of the Ecclesiastical Committee and one volume relating to the proselytes, i.e. those newly converted from Catholicism to Protestantism. In the early period, at least, it seems that applicants had to produce a certificate to attest that they had taken the sacrament according to the Church of England. The grants given are usually divided into lists according to the social status of the recipients: 'Persons of Quality', the 'middle condition' and the 'meaner sort'. The amount of money disbursed depended on the category into which individuals fell.

A catalogue of the records in the Huguenot Library of the Royal Bounty (though not of individual applicants or recipients) has been published by the Huguenot Society (HSQS, Vol. LI). The history of the funds and the whereabouts of various copies of them is a complicated one, detailed in the introduction to this catalogue. In 1988 a two-year project was set up to extract details of all the recipients between 1686 and 1709 and computerise them to enable analysis. A print-out of the computerised records, arranged alphabetically, is held in the Huguenot Library. These are not transcripts of the records: information has been selected according to predetermined fields to make statistical analysis possible, though they do cover the main period of Huguenot immigration. They are easy to use and include information such as where the individuals were living, their places of origin, number of children and even social class.

At the back of the Acts of the Consistory of the church of Thorpe-le-Soken are notes about the distribution of money from the Royal Bounty between 1699 and 1763. These are described in HSQS, Vol. LI, but have not been transcribed in this publication.

Schools

One of the major ways of preserving a culture is through education. In London the Threadneedle Street church set up two schools for the children of Huguenots and those of Huguenot descent. Keith Le May has done extensive research on the history of these schools and their pupils and his work has been published in the *Proceedings*.

It was first proposed to establish a school in 1681, but it was not until 1719 that enough money was raised to set up a school in Spitalfields. Boys and girls were educated separately. Later in 1747 another school was opened in Westminster. By 1803 the Spitalfields establishment was in trouble and very few pupils remained. It was decided to close the building and to pay for the children to attend independent schools. The boys were sent to one being run by one of the church's erstwhile deacons. The girls went to be educated in the home of their former schoolmistress. After the boys' teacher died in 1827 his pupils were transferred to a school in Bethnal Green, run by a Mr Hudson, who may or may not have been of Huguenot descent. By 1852, the girls were also being educated there and the total number of children was down to around ten. The headmaster was a Mr Sherwood, so it seems unlikely that they were still being educated in French, as the authorities originally intended. The last invoice for their education among the church records is in 1863.

The Westminster school managed to retain teaching in the French language and instruction in the Huguenots' religious tenets for much longer, because it also took the children of French people from the community in Soho. There is still a fund providing support for the education of those of Huguenot descent.

Charity Apprenticeships

Once pupils had left the schools, they needed to earn their livings. To teach their skills, masters asked for a sum of money, called a premium. If they were members of the livery companies of the City of London they could charge hefty amounts, as those who completed apprenticeships with them would be entitled to claim the Freedom of the City, with all the privileges that brought. However, even the lesser sums charged by those who were not members of the livery companies would still be out of the question for poor parents. A number of people left money in their wills to fund apprenticeships. Étienne Seignoret and Stephen Mounier left legacies for apprenticeships administered by the French Hospital, which also used other legacies to pay premiums. Madeleine Marie Delaigle left money to the Society of Saintonge and Augoumois to fund apprenticeships. The names of the boys and girls who were apprenticed by these various funds and the names of their masters are scattered among a number of records. They have been brought together and published by Keith Le May in the *Proceedings*.

156					
Apprenticeships under the Will of Stephen Mounier					
		Apprentice	Master		
1832	November	3 Clements	Butfoy	£12 .	£12 .
1833					
	February	2 Griffiths	Green	12. —	12
1834					
	February	1 Stringer	Carter	12.	
	May	3 Medyer	Wells	13. —	24
1835					
	August	1 Elley	Ward	12.	12. —
1836				/	
	January	9 Vardon	Leech	12	
	Septemb	3 Deboos	Perkins	12	
	Decemb	3 Planck	Guibert	12. —	36
1837					
	February	4 Stringer	Carter	8	
		Brown	Warren	12	

Stephen Mounier provided a legacy to pay for the apprenticeship of young people of Huguenot descent.

Even today, the various legacies are used by the directors of the French Hospital to help aspiring craftsmen and women of Huguenot descent, usually to enable them to buy tools to pursue their trade.

Friendly Societies

From the late seventeenth century groups of people banded together, paying in a small weekly sum of money to provide a fund from which those who fell on hard times through unemployment or illness could draw. They became known as 'Friendly Societies'. Initially the government looked on them with great suspicion: it was thought they might be cover for subversive political activity and it was not until 1793 that they were recognised by an Act of Parliament. Long before that, however, a number had been set up by Huguenot migrants.

They were organised on regional lines: the first known one was established in 1683 as the Société des Enfants de Nîmes (Society of the Children of Nîmes) and its members were drawn from the area around that city in the south of France. It was followed by the Société des Parisiens (later the Huguenot Friendly Benefit Society) in 1687. Others based on regions include:

- Société de la Provence de Normandie (1703–1962) (Society of the Province of Normandy)
- Société de Lintot (1708–1964) (Society of Lintot)
- Société de St Onge et Augoumois (1701–1872) (Society of Saintonge and Augoumois)
- Société du Dauphiné (Society of the Dauphiné)
- Société des Provinces du Poitou, Xaintonge, et Pays d'Aunix (Society of the Provinces of Poitou, Saintonge, and the Region of Aunix)
- Société du Poitou et du Loudunois (Society of Poitou and Loudunois)
- Society of High and Low Normandy (established 1764)
- Les Méridionaux was a society for those from the south of France and is known from a single reference to a celebration in Paddington in 1715
- The Society of Picards and Walloons is also known from a single reference; in 1799 it said that it was a friendly society, not a political organisation; it met at the Turkish Slave public house (now the Jolly Butchers) in Brick Lane

A non-regional society was the Bachelors, established in Spitalfields in 1697, for French Protestants and their descendants. Another, simply called the Friendly Society, set up in 1720, was not restricted to people from a particular region of France: instead they had to live within three miles of St Matthew's Church, Bethnal Green, where there were substantial numbers of Huguenot families.

Wednesday January 1ˢᵗ 1851

Received of Mᵣ Jolit. Three Pounds as a gift from the Saint Onge Society Chauvet's fund

£ 3 . 0 . 0   S L Vitou

S.L. Vitou received regular payments from the Society of Saintonge and Augoumois.

The HL holds full records of the Society of the Province of Normandy and records from 1785 to 1872 of the Society of Saintonge and Angoumois. The papers of the Society of Lintot are privately owned but copies of some of the papers have been deposited in the HL.

The records of the Huguenot Friendly Benefit Society 1797–1912 are held in LMA (CLC/144), but earlier records have not survived. LMA also contains the records of other friendly societies in Spitalfields and Bethnal Green to which people of Huguenot descent may have belonged. These are the Friendly Brothers' Provident Loan Society, the Friendly Loan Society, the Diamond Friendly Loan Society and the Friendly Artisans Loan Society.

The whereabouts of any surviving records of the other societies have not yet been discovered. Although both TNA and the Registry of Friendly Societies hold the papers of many societies, none of the Huguenot ones seem to be among them.

Wills

Copies of some wills, especially those which left legacies either to the French Hospital or another Huguenot body, are held in the HL and are detailed in the catalogues. As well as creating pedigrees, Henry Wagner trawled through the copies of wills enrolled in the Prerogative Court of Canterbury (PCC) until 1858. He extracted the names of those whom he knew were or seemed to be Huguenots and made a detailed abstract, or digest, of the contents of these wills. His notebooks, held in the Huguenot Library, were edited by Dorothy North and published by the Huguenot Society (HSQS, Vol. LX: Huguenot Wills and Administrations in England and Ireland 1617–1849). Ms North also produced a complete index to everyone mentioned, not just the testators, published as a companion volume. However, Mr Wagner relied on names that seemed to be Huguenot so they are not complete. Sometimes his omissions are inexplicable: the will of Isaac Bonouvrier, for example, is not in his collection, although other members of the family are included. The wills of Isaac and Joseph Montellier are also omitted, although their surnames are obviously French and they were, in fact, of Huguenot origin. Those whose names had been translated or corrupted into something that appears to be British are also probably not included.

As these are abstracts of the originals, they do not include everything in the testators' wills and the researcher should look them up on TNA's website, where copies from the PCC can be downloaded for a fee.

Other Foreign Churches

Most ports have places of worship for mariners from various countries. London, being the largest centre of commerce, has always had a significant migrant population, some of whom set up their own churches. It may be that family stories of French or Huguenot ancestry may actually relate to people who came to London for economic purposes and settled here. The Dutch Church of Austin Friars, initially intended for religious refugees, later served (and still serves) the general Dutch population of London.

From the late seventeenth century, a few individuals from Germany are found in the records of the French churches in London. They may have come from Huguenot refugee families. The first church to serve the German-speaking community in London, the Hamburg Lutheran Church, was established in 1669 and others followed, so some Protestant migrants of Huguenot origin may have joined these churches, although as most would have been French-speaking they are more likely to be found in the French churches' records.

A Swiss church was established in London in 1760. The records remain in the church's office.

A Swedish church, mainly used by seafarers, was established in London in 1710. The records are still held in the church office in London, with a copy in the library of the Anglo-German Family History Society.

There was a Danish church in London, established in 1692, but no records before 1880 survive.

Because those of Walloon, Dutch and Huguenot ancestry were scattered across Europe, it is also possible that their assimilated descendants later came to England, long after the persecutions had ceased and records of them may be found in these 'foreign' churches.

Research Overseas

Once you have discovered where your family originated from in France, the Netherlands or the Low Countries, or from the country in which they spent time before re-migrating, there may be a certain amount that you can do on the internet or in specialist libraries. The first port of call should, of course, be the Huguenot Library but there are other possible sources. The Institute of Historical Research at the University of London, for example, has numerous guides to archives, local histories and histories of Protestantism in all the countries of Europe. Its holdings are not confined to academic works. Among its miscellaneous documents, for example, it has a copy of a typescript of a list of Protestants in Rouen and Quevilly, extracted by Pierre Legendre from documents in the Departmental Archives and from the municipal library of Rouen. This contains baptisms, marriage and burials from 1609 to 1677 and a list of permissions to bury, 1746–88. The library of the Society of Genealogists also has a substantial collection of overseas records.

There is a lot of material on the internet. Records are being increasing digitised. Even if you are able to surmount the problem of old handwriting and spelling to copy entries exactly, the language can be a further difficulty. Luckily there are volunteers who offer to translate, for example, from Dutch to English for free. You can try the website called Random Acts of Genealogical Kindness.

Unless you are very lucky and are connected to a well-documented family, once you have exhausted the sources in Britain, you will need to decide whether you are going to hire a professional genealogist with knowledge of both the language and the specialist records or travel overseas to the records and do the research yourself. How far you can or want to go to pursue their histories overseas depends on a number of factors. The first, of course, is how confident you are about the language. Although most people working in overseas archives have at least a working knowledge of English (and almost all Dutch and German people in official positions have an excellent command of the language), you cannot expect busy archivists and librarians to do your work for you.

If, however, you have a moderate grasp of the language, you will find it useful to read guides to researching family history published in the particular country you plan to visit. These are useful, both to find out what records there are and how they are organised and to introduce you to the specialist vocabulary used by genealogists and record offices there. Basic advice on researching in overseas archives and libraries is given in Chapter 6.

If you decide not to go yourself, the alternative is to hire a local researcher. The Huguenot Society has a genealogist based in France who can undertake work there. Details are on the website. Local record offices in the country where your ancestors originated should be able to suggest people who can help you.

Even if you cannot undertake a research trip, you might like to visit your ancestors' home town or village while on holiday. Most parts of regional France that had a strong Huguenot connection now have a dedicated museum – these and the ones in Germany and Belgium are included in the Addresses and Websites section at the back of this book.

Chapter 5

GENERAL SOURCES

Of course Huguenots could not live entirely within their own communities. They had to deal with indigenous people on a regular basis. Over the generations, they were assimilated into the general population. Any standard book on genealogy will detail the other sources of family history, like service in the armed forces, taxes, property deeds and insurance, trade directories and the myriad records where occupations and activities are recorded. (S&N Genealogy Supplies are the biggest suppliers in Britain of printed church registers and these other sources on CD-ROM.) This chapter deals only with the main places to consider. Many people will have reached the point of suspecting Huguenot forebears by following the usual routes into their ancestry but the sources below will serve as a checklist and may give ideas for other avenues of research.

Church Records

As Huguenots were absorbed into the general population, they moved from attending their own churches into the Church of England or other nonconformist denominations and sects. It might be expected that those from conformist congregations would be more likely to join the Church of England and nonconformist congregation members would be drawn to the various English nonconformist denominations and sects. This is not a hard-and-fast rule: as people were assimilated, more were drawn into mainstream Anglicanism so this should be the first port of call for researchers.

Church of England parish registers and records

As well as its spiritual role, the Church of England was in charge of local government until the middle of the nineteenth century, when these functions were taken over by lay bodies or the state.

Parishes collected taxes, known as rates, from property owners and holders for a variety of purposes, such as the maintenance of roads and the support of the poor and sick. Huguenots will be found in the parish's rate-books, along with the sums for which they were assessed, which will give an indication of their income as well as their addresses. Although there were specific charities for people of Huguenot descent, like the French Hospital in London, others who fell on hard times, particularly outside London, will be found in the standard sources for the administration of the Poor Laws, such as the distribution of money or recording the inmates of workhouses.

As most Huguenot churches did not have burial grounds, individuals might be interred in their local parish churchyard and entries will be found in their registers.

Nonconformists

Before the Civil Wars and the Commonwealth period (1642–60) Dissenters faced persecution so kept few records in case they could be used against them. From the 1640s, however, the Puritan regime of Oliver Cromwell (himself a Separatist) favoured them. During this period of religious and political upheaval a number of other sects formed: the Muggletonians, the Diggers, the Ranters, the Fifth Monarchy Men. Most of them expected the imminent end of the world and the fulfilment of the prophesies in the Book of the Revelation of St John, so they kept few records. The majority of these groups remained small and on the fringes of society. After 1660 most of their adherents returned to more mainstream nonconformity or even to the Church of England.

On the restoration of Charles II, nonconformists again faced opposition and persecution. Various Acts of Parliament were passed to control them but the Huguenots were a comparatively privileged section of the non-conformist population, as they were given the legal right to practise their religion by a succession of monarchs and were exempt from these Acts. In the period up to 1689, Walloons and Dutch refugees, or their descendants, who left their churches to join one of these dissenting groups, are unlikely to be recorded, unless they fell foul of the law in some way and are noted in Quarter Sessions records, church courts or returns of non-Anglicans made by individual parishes. These should be found in county record offices or in TNA.

Other Nonconformist Denominations and Sects

Quakers

The Religious Society of Friends (Quakers) was founded in 1643. They kept good records from the beginning. Friends Library in London has an extensive library of their history and records of their meetings all over the country.

Methodists

The Methodists began in the mid-eighteenth century as a reform movement within the Church of England and did not formally separate until the early nineteenth century. They split into various sub-groups, some of which did not last long and reunited with the mainstream. Others ultimately found their home with the Congregationalists. The main ones were the Countess of Huntingdon's Connexion and Primitive Methodism.

Sandemanians

This movement was founded by John Glas in Scotland in 1730, where they were known as Glasites. Some people of Huguenot descent may have joined his movement there. His son-in-law Robert Sandeman took over the leadership of his church and moved to London in 1760, where he attracted followers. It is by his name that this sect is usually known in England and America, where Sandeman moved in 1764. As they did not practise baptism, family historians face problems in reconstructing their Sandemanian ancestry. No congregations survive and when the last descendant of Robert Sandeman died, the records were deposited with the University of Dundee.

Don Steel's *Sources for Nonconformist Genealogy and Family History* is an excellent introduction to the history of the various denominations mentioned above and the kinds of records that they kept, along with accounts of other more obscure sects, such as the Inghamites, who were confined to the north of England, and so are unlikely to have attracted Huguenots. His work also contains a section on the Huguenots themselves. The Society of Genealogists' *My Ancestors Were . . .* series has booklets on English Presbyterians/Unitarians, Baptists, Congregationalists, Methodists and Inghamites. Each has a brief overview of the denomination's history and lists of the known congregations, their dates and where their surviving records are now deposited. There are of course numerous other works on the histories of nonconformist denominations.

The French Prophets

One of the short-lived sects that attracted a few Huguenot converts was a movement known as the French Prophets. They were a millenarian sect, predicting the end of the world. In 1706 three 'prophets' from south-west France appeared in London. It might be expected that their fellow countrymen would have been drawn to them and indeed some of the first followers were French. Their main attraction, however, was to native Britons. Only a few Huguenots were among their congregations. By 1712 the Prophets had tiny groups of followers scattered over southern

England, some in towns which had established Huguenot churches, like Bristol and Colchester. There were none in the north or in Wales. There was a group of twenty-one followers in Dublin. They had some success in Scotland and in mainland Europe. The movement lasted in Britain until the 1730s, and for a longer time in France, where it had its roots. Its history has been described in Hillel Schwartz's *The French Prophets*, which contains a list of all its followers in Britain. Whether the British Huguenot followers returned to their old congregations or joined other denominations is not yet known.

Dr Williams's Library

Dr Williams's Library is the major research library of English Protestant nonconformity. It was established under the will of a Presbyterian minister Dr Daniel Williams (*c.* 1643–1716), whose second wife, Jane Guill, was the daughter of a refugee Huguenot merchant. Entries in Church of England parish registers were accepted as legal documents but nonconformist records had no such status. Some non-Anglican congregations' records were not well kept because ministers carried the notes around with them. To overcome these problems, the three Dissenting churches (Congregationalists, English Presbyterians and Baptists) decided to establish a

Dr Williams's Library in Gordon Square, London

general register of the births of children. The scheme was not limited to those belonging to the three denominations – anyone could avail themselves of this service, even Anglicans. It was started in 1742/3 and records were held in the library of Dr Williams. People would send duplicate certificates, signed by the parents and friends of a child. One was kept at the library, where it was entered in a book, and the other returned to the parents with confirmation of the registration. The register was closed in 1837, when national registration was introduced, and was surrendered to the government shortly after. It is now in TNA, but a copy is held in the library.

In addition, the library holds a number of other useful sources of nonconformist history, including some church minute books, many predating any registers that might have been kept and mentioning baptisms and deaths. Lists of church members have also been deposited there. The main source of genealogical information for nonconformists in the library, however, is the collection of magazines published by the three Dissenting denominations, which began at the end of the eighteenth century. They frequently give obituaries of ministers and other members of congregations. Family historians with ministers in their ancestry will also find biographical notes about them and, if they put their sermons and other theological thoughts into print, their published works.

Marriage Licences

After 1753 only marriages which took place in an Anglican parish church or by Quaker or Jewish ceremonies were legal. Even before that, however, nonconformist as well as conformist Huguenots did marry in their parish churches because their records were proof of marriage that would be easily accepted in a court of law. Both before and after 1753, nonconformists preferred to be married by licence rather than by banns, which were called in the local parish church for three weeks before the actual ceremony. Licences were issued either by bishops or archbishops. Lists of licences have been published or are held in CROs.

Many parishes with a small population did not carry out enough ceremonies to give the incumbent an adequate living so the minister supplemented his income by being willing to marry those who, for one reason or another, did not want their nuptials to be public. The parish church of Little Ilford in Essex was isolated, set in open fields on the edge of marshland. In some years there were only one or two baptisms and no burials, but there were comparatively numerous marriages. On 4 April 1738 Peter Bonouvrier, from a Huguenot family, married Elizabeth Glover there. They both travelled from the City of London for the ceremony and had no connection with the area. She was the widow of one of his business partners. On marriage, her deceased husband's share of the business became her new husband's. The motive for the secrecy seems to have been to conceal from the remaining partner Peter Bonouvrier's acquisition of a controlling share of the business.

If a marriage cannot be found where it would be expected, it is worth checking whether there were any of these churches conducting a disproportionate number of marriages in the area.

There were also a number of churches that fell outside the jurisdiction of the local bishop and claimed the right to issue their own licences. Marriages under these conditions are known as 'irregular' marriages. The most notorious place, however, was the area around the Fleet Prison, where clandestine marriages were conducted. Clergymen waited there, ready to marry couples with no questions asked and no licences demanded. The original Fleet registers are held in TNA and have been transcribed by Mark Herber in three volumes: *Clandestine Marriages in the Chapel and Rules of the Fleet Prison 1680-1754*, also available on CD-ROM from S&N. They do not, of course, mention origins or religious affiliations but among them are a number of people with names that are obviously French, and among these may be Huguenots who, for whatever reason, wanted to conceal their weddings.

Burial Records

Many Huguenots were interred in their local parish churchyards, usually without any mention of their religious affiliation. A few Anglican ministers, however, were unwilling to bury nonconformists or they might not read a service over someone who was not a member of the Church of England. Since burial registers are records of services rather than events, nonconforming Huguenots may not appear in parish registers even though they were buried in the churchyard. Sometimes details of fees paid for burials will appear in the parish's churchwarden's accounts so these should be consulted. Burial day books, which record all burials in a churchyard, have not survived in great numbers but should always be investigated. More usefully, some Church of England clerks noted the burials of all their parishioners, even if they took place elsewhere.

There were some private burial grounds, like Mount Nod in Wandsworth. In Maidstone, Kent, in 1760 102 children died in a smallpox epidemic and were buried 'out of town'. Though this event was mentioned in the parish register, the names were not recorded.

Victoria Park Cemetery, between Bethnal Green and Bow in the East End of London, was never consecrated and it was notorious for all kinds of abuses. Eventually it was converted into a recreation ground, called Meath Gardens. Few of the records, if any, that were kept of these private grounds have survived. In London Bunhill Fields was established in 1665 specifically for nonconformists who did not want to be buried in Anglican

Bunhill Fields in the City of London was opened in 1665 as a nonconformist burial ground.

churchyards. By 1840 it was full, but it was not officially closed until 1852; records from 1713 to 1852 survive. The original registers of Bunhill Fields are in TNA and online. There is also an index to the burials and a filmed copy of the registers in LMA. Abney Park Cemetery in Stoke Newington, north London, opened in 1840 and became another major burial site for nonconformists. The French Hospital used the City of London Cemetery at Aldersbrook in the parish of Little Ilford. It appears as 'Ilford' in the Hospital's records. This was opened in 1856.

Apprenticeship Records

As noted before, many Huguenots were artisans. They faced a lot of opposition from indigenous Britons afraid of competition from them, and local guilds often passed regulations limiting their opportunities. There is a very useful summary of the kind of ordinances that the Corporation of London passed against foreign craftsmen in Irene Scouladi's introduction to the *Returns of Strangers in the Metropolis* (HSQS, Vol. LVII, also on CD-ROM). However, these restrictions did not apply outside the Square Mile and many Huguenots are found living and working outside the City.

Master craftsmen might well become freemen of their city or borough and records relating to them will be found in county and local record offices. In the City of London, the city livery company records are held either in the Guildhall Library (GL) or are still with the individual companies. SoG publishes a series of booklets *My Ancestor Was . . .* which detail how a profession was organised and regulated, what records relate to it and where to access them. The most useful to someone tracing Huguenot ancestry is probably *My Ancestors Were Freemen of the City of London*, but most trades and professions will contain someone of French or Dutch ancestry.

Apprenticeships were private arrangements so it is rare for the original documents to survive but City of London livery companies contain records of those apprenticed and those who gained their freedom, whether by completing an apprenticeship or simply by paying a fee. Records are either with the company itself, such as the Drapers, or in the GL, such as the Weavers, and many have been published. The SoG Library holds a collection of indentures between 1641 and 1888.

The East End of London is mainly associated with silk-weaving and many Huguenots and their descendants in the Spitalfields area followed the trade. Extracts from the Weavers' Company records have been published by the Huguenot Society (HSQS, Vol. XXXIII). The records distinguish between native-born members and those who were foreign-born.

However, Huguenots worked in a variety of other trades, so records of their apprenticeships and the apprentices that they themselves took will be found in the records of the various livery companies. Between 1710 and 1808, there was a tax on premiums over 1s paid to masters to teach an apprentice and these records, which actually go up to 1811, are held in TNA in IR1/1-19 and IT1/41-5. Apprenticeships of a child to its father and Poor Law apprenticeships were exempt, so not everyone appears in these records. There is a factsheet on the TNA website. Digitised copies of the government records from 1711 to 1754 have been put on CD-ROM by Archive Books, but are no longer available to buy. An index for 1710–74 is online at www.findmypast.com. Copies of this index are also held by TNA, SoG and GL. Cliff Webb is extracting and publishing through the SoG a series of booklets detailing London apprentices by company.

Military Men

People of Dutch, Walloon and Huguenot descent served in both the army and navy, and records relating to them will be found in the standard sources for the armed forces. There were a few Huguenot regiments, which had largely been disbanded by 1689, but the largest band of Huguenot soldiers were brought together when the deposed king James II landed in

Ireland in 1689, supported by Louis XIV. James was intent on recovering his throne, by now occupied by his son–in-law William III, and thousands of Irishmen flocked to fight for him, as he was a Roman Catholic. William III sent out appeals to Huguenots all over Europe to unite with him and responses came from England, France, the Netherlands and Germany. Along with Britons of the standing army, and, surprisingly, the blessing of the Pope, they defeated James, with the campaign culminating at the Battle of the Boyne in 1690. Many of the veterans settled in Ireland, particularly in Portarlington (see Chapter 2).

It was, however, in the War of the Spanish Succession (1702–13) against Louis XIV, the Seven Years War (1756–63) and the French and Napoleonic Wars (1793–1815) that soldiers and naval men of Huguenot descent made the biggest contribution to defeating the native land of their ancestors. In the HL, there is an index compiled by Hilton Jones to Huguenot army officers and the *Proceedings* contain many articles on the contributions made by Huguenots to the armed forces.

Crime

Huguenots were both perpetrators and victims of crime; they also sat on juries. There are many published sources of information about records, like David Hawkings's *Criminal Ancestors*. The best starting point for those with London ancestors is *The Whole Proceedings on the King's Commissions of the Peace, Oyez and Terminer, and Gaol Delivery held for the City of London,* etc., usually known as the *Proceedings*. This started as a publication containing summaries of trials at the Old Bailey. Later, the evidence given was taken down in full in shorthand and transcribed. Transcripts (and images of the original publications) between 1674 and 1913 are online. This site also contains associated documents, like descriptions of those executed, written and published by the chaplain of Newgate Prison, known as the Ordinary's Accounts. It is easy to run names through the keyword search, and this will turn up any mention of a name anywhere in the whole documents, whether defendant, prosecutor, witness, member of the jury or simply mentioned in evidence. Cases which did not get as far as the Old Bailey may be found in either Sessions of the Peace for Westminster, the City of London or Middlesex (in LMA). There is, unfortunately, no equivalent outside the capital, where records will be found in Quarter Sessions records in CROs, and assize records, in TNA. County and local newspapers usually at least mentioned cases.

Wills

Until 1858, when proving wills was taken over the by state, the Prerogative Court of Canterbury (PCC) was the highest court to prove wills in England

and Wales. It was used by those who had property in more than one diocese and also had jurisdiction over British colonies, including America until 1783, if the testator had property in both the colony and in Britain. People who died at sea on a British ship also had their wills proved here, these usually being Royal Navy sailors. Administrations were granted in the case of people who had died intestate and were usually given to either the spouse or a child of the deceased.

However there were lower church courts dealing with probate. The wills of people who had property and chattels in a single archdeaconry could be proved in the archdiocesan court. If they had property in more than one archdeaconry, wills were proved in the bishop's court, usually called the consistory or commissary court. Archdeaconry and consistory court wills are usually found in the local CRO, but there are a few dioceses which maintain a separate record office. An index to the wills in the commissary and archdeaconry courts of London can be found in London Signatures on the LMA website and the wills themselves are on microfilm there.

The details of courts given above should be regarded as a guideline. Wills were not automatically proved in the court where they might be expected. It is clear from the PCC wills that many of the testators had little to leave and an archdeaconry court would have been the most appropriate (and cheapest) option. There seems to have been a misapprehension that money deposited in the Bank of England was regarded as property in a separate diocese by those living outside the City, so it is a good place to look for relatively wealthy ancestors.

In most cases, proving a will or obtaining an administration was a quick and routine process, so a delay might imply some kind of problem. Sometimes, of course, if a person died overseas it might take time for the news to reach England. Those who disputed the provisions of a will had to pursue their cases in the Church courts, so these should be checked if there is a long gap between the death of an individual in Britain and the proving or his or her will.

Some wills made by employees of the East India Company (EIC) were proved locally and are deposited in the Oriental and India Office Library at the British Library. The EIC held a monopoly of dealings with India, China and East Asia from 1600 to 1858 and a number of people of Huguenot ancestry are known to have been involved with it.

Before 1882, wives' property was automatically transferred to their husband on marriage, unless protected by a trust. Only a few wills of married women, like that of Magdalen Mariette, wife of Paul Dufour, exist. Her will, presumably made in case her husband predeceased her, was never proved but he decided to honour her wishes when she died before him. It has been preserved in the Huguenot Library among the papers of the French Hospital, of which Paul Dufour was a director. The Dufours were childless and Magdalen's will is a treasure trove of genealogical information, as she left legacies to many of her relatives. Paul Dufour, whose will Henry Wagner included in his collection, also left numerous legacies to his relatives.

The original wills proved in the Prerogative Court of Armagh (PCA) were lost when the Irish Public Record Office, housed in Four Courts, Dublin, was destroyed by protestors against British rule in 1922. Henry Wagner's work on wills is therefore of particular value to those with Huguenot ancestors in Ireland.

In Scotland the law relating to wills was, and still is, different from that in England and Wales. There were laid-down rules of who should automatically inherit land and buildings. Only moveable property, like cash, furniture, jewellery, etc., could be left as the testator chose. This means that far fewer wills were proved in Scotland: the family often sorted things out amongst themselves. Wills, called testaments, were proved in commissariats, roughly the equivalents of dioceses, until 1823 and thereafter by local sheriff's courts until 1876, when a national system was introduced.

Inquests

Inquests are a little-used source of information about family history and Huguenots occasionally died in circumstances that triggered an inquest just like anyone else. As respectable members of the middle classes, they would also have been summoned to sit on juries. An inquest was also supposed to be held on everyone who died in prison. Since people could also be imprisoned for debt until 1869, the likelihood is that a number of Huguenots will be among those who died in the noxious conditions of the prisons.

Tracking down inquest records can be a tricky process, since the jurisdiction of individual coroners might not be where expected and relatively few records have survived. Newspapers frequently reported proceedings, so it is always worth looking through newspapers for a month or so after any family member died in case there was an inquest.

There is a Gibson Guide to the whereabouts of surviving inquest documents as well as those that have been published, arranged by county. The Gibson Guides, booklets written by Jeremy Gibson, sometimes with a co-editor, list the holdings, county by county, of record offices in England and Wales relating to a particular kind of record, e.g. land tax assessments, coroners' records, electoral registers. The earlier ones were published by the Federation of Family History Societies but more up-to-date editions are now produced by the Family History Group.

101

Chapter 6

SETTLEMENTS IN MAINLAND EUROPE

In the various European countries each has the usual structure of national archives, relating to the government's business: regional or provincial records and local records. Where church registers and other records are held varies according to the country. Remember that, in addition to church records, there are the usual documents that genealogists use: records of the armed forces, land records, taxes, criminal records and, of course, wills. The Church of Latter-Day Saints has filmed many (if not most) of the surviving church registers around the continent. Entries from them are being put on the International Genealogical Index (IGI) and the films themselves can be ordered through their Family History Centers.

Tracing Ancestors in France

Before the French Revolution, which started in 1789, the records are very different from those created after 1792 and the more radical changes later made under Napoleon, although these need not concern us as by then all Huguenots had left France. From 1559, Protestant pastors were recommended by their own church to keep records of baptisms and the names of the child's parents. In 1563 an official edict required magistrates to register the births of Protestants in their region, but this was not effectively observed. After the Edict of Nantes in 1598 brought a measure of toleration, Protestant pastors started to keep registers of baptisms, marriages and burials. From the start of renewed persecution in the middle of the eighteenth century up to the Revocation in 1685, the registers became less well kept because it was dangerous to record information that might be used against church members. After the Revocation, all ceremonies had to take place in Catholic churches. Protestants were enjoined to obey lawful authority, so their baptisms, marriages and burials will be found in the Catholic records. This was often under protest and there are many records relating to those who refused to conform or to those whom the authorities suspected of insincerity. In fact most information on Protestant families in times of persecution comes from the authorities who were oppressing them.

Location of records relating to Huguenots

France is no longer divided into provinces: it is now divided into depart-ments, each with its own record office. There are also some *archives communales* (community archives) and a few records remain in the *mairie* (mayor's office). In France, wills were lodged in the local solicitor's office and, although legislation was passed in 1928 and 1976 requiring any will over 125 years old to be deposited in the departmental archives, not all have been discovered: they still turn up from time to time in solicitors' offices and other places, their existence and place of storage having been long forgotten.

Gildas Bernard's *Les familles protestantes en France: XVIe siècle–1792: guide des recherches biographiques et généalogiques* (Protestant Families in France: 16th century–1792: guide to bibliographic and genealogical research) is the most comprehensive guide to the whereabouts of sources of informa-tion about Protestants in pre-Revolutionary France. The book is arranged by modern-day department and each section is preceded by a brief summary of Protestantism in the area. Then follows a list of surviving records and where they are located, whether in the departmental archives, the National Archives in Paris, or other record offices or libraries. There is also a bibliog-raphy. Most departmental archives have their own detailed guides, but Bernard has selected those records relevant to Protestants. His manual is very easy to use, once you know from where your family originated.

If your ancestor, for example, came from the town of Civray in the old region of Poitou, you will need to look on a modern map to find its present-day department, which is Vienne. Turning to the chapter on Vienne in Bernard's guide, we discover that in the departmental archives there are some fragments of Protestant registers from 1674 and 1680 relating to Civray. There are also numerous lists of fugitives and new converts relating to the whole region of Poitou, a list of the girl children of Protestants and new converts sent to 'the Christian Union of Poitiers' and abjurations of Protestants made in Catholic churches. In the same record office, there are notes on the legal proceedings and judgements against those converts who contravened the ordinances of their new religion and documents detailing the goods seized from the premises of fugitives who had fled from the town. The Bibliothèque de la Société de l'histoire du Protestantism français (Library of the History of French Protestantism Society) in Paris has some studies of Protestantism in Poitiers and the papers of a couple of pastors. The bibliography lists various books and also two published family histories.

The Dutch Republic

Over the years many thousands of refugees from France and the Low Countries sought asylum in the Dutch Republic – some put the figure as high as 100,000 – and they formed a large proportion of the population there. The long, and generally amicable, relationship between England and the Netherlands meant that there were Huguenot family links between the two countries. As the *témoignage* records of the Threadneedle Street church in London show, at least 1,500 came to England in the period 1669–1789. The church registers also show that most of the French congregations in London had at least a few members born in the Netherlands, such as Henri Guillaume Vial 'Hollandois' who made his reconnaissance (recognition of his 'fault' in converting to Catholicism) at the Church of the Savoy in March 1700. Outside London, there were negligible numbers of Dutch people attending the French churches.

Amsterdam

This town was a major centre of Walloon and later Huguenot migration. Soon after 1578, when Amsterdam converted to Protestantism, the former chapel of a monastery was put at the disposal of French-speaking Protestant refugees. This Waalsekerk (Walloon church) still conducts a service in French every Sunday. Admissions to the Freedom of the City of Amsterdam rose from 344 in 1575–9 to 2,768 in 1615–19, and most of those were migrants bringing skills and wealth. By 1609–11 Walloons made up a third of the highest income tax payers of the city's inhabitants. After the Revocation in 1685, sixteen ministers banished from France went to Amsterdam and some 200 went to other towns in the United Provinces. By 1700, up to a quarter of the population in Amsterdam was of French origin. The community was large enough to need an orphanage, the Walenweeshuis; they set up bookshops and printing presses, producing publications which spread news of scientific, political, cultural and, naturally, theological matters throughout Europe.

Rotterdam

The Waalsekerk in Rotterdam was established in 1585 but at the start of the dragonnades in France the number of refugees grew swiftly. Between 1680 and 1705 the congregation grew to more than 440 members, totalling 1,560 people, including children and other family members who were not formal members of the church. There was also a Flemish Reformed church in Rotterdam at this time, and the two were intermittently in contact, mainly over matters of doctrine or charity.

The Acts of the Consistory of this church, *Le consistoire de l'Église wallonne de Rotterdam 1681–1706* (Consistory of the Walloon Church of Rotterdam 1681–1706) (Honoré Champion, Paris, 2008), edited by Hubert Bost, in the series 'La Vie Protestante' (The Protestant Life), are largely to do with church governance and money matters – finances being especially important when refugees were constantly arriving. The other matter they obsessively discussed was the conflict between their pastor, Pierre Jurieu (1637 1713), and Pierre Bayle (1647 1706). Bayle was the son of a Protestant minister in France and had a turbulent religious career. For a short while, he abjured Protestantism for Catholicism, then returned to the faith of his childhood. This relapse made him a heretic and he had to flee to Geneva. Later he was appointed Professor of Philosophy at the Protestant University of Sedan in Northern France. When the university was suppressed in 1681 he had to flee again, this time to Rotterdam, where he took up a post at the École Illustre (Distinguished School). His publications on Calvinist history and doctrine were widely admired, except by Pastor Pierre Jurieu, a colleague who had also been at the university in Sedan and had published similar works. Due to Jurieu's criticisms of Bayle's writings, the latter was deprived of his chair in 1693. Inevitably the church's congregation was drawn into their professional and personal quarrels. Mr Bost was primarily interested in the implications of their theological quarrels, so transcribed only the section of the consistory minutes of this period.

Other communities in the Netherlands

In addition to these two major centres, French-speaking refugees established churches and communities all over the Netherlands. Those that survive are in Arnhem, Breda, Delft, The Hague, Dordrecht, Groningue, Haarlem, Leiden, Maastricht, Middelburg, Utrecht and Zwolle. Others, now closed, were at Aardenburg (where there was a combined Dutch and Walloon church), Amersfoort, Axel et Philippine Balk, Bergen op Zoom, Blégny, Bolsward, Brielle, Cadzand (established in 1686), Dalheim, Deventer, Dwingelo, Enkhuizen, Franeker, Goes, Gorinchem, Gouda, Grave, Groede, Harderwijk, Hattem, 's-Hertogenbosch, Heusden, Hodiment et Petit-Rechain, Hoorn, Ijzendijke, Kampen, Leeuwarden, Limbourg, Middelburg, Montfoort, Naarden, Nimigen, Noordwijk, Olne, Églises de l'Olive, Oostburg, Sas van Gent, Schiedam, Sluis, Sneek, Tholen, Tiel, Vaals, Veere, Vlissingen, Weesp, Zaltbommel, Zierikzee and Zutphen.

The Acts of various consistories of the Walloon churches have been published as *Livre des Actes des Églises Wallonnes aux Pays-Bas 1601–1697* (Book of the Acts of the Walloon Churches in the Netherlands 1601–1697). These Acts are largely to do with church discipline, theological questions and the relationships between the various churches: they do not deal with the everyday transgressions of congregation members. They will therefore be of use to those with pastors or other church authorities in their ancestry, or to those interested in the history of the churches. Occasionally there are accounts in the form of expenses to attend synods or personal requests – such as one from a minister wanting to leave his congregation – that give some personal information. Most are in French, some in Dutch and some in Latin, the lingua franca of the period.

Tracing ancestors in the Netherlands

Until 1811, registers of baptisms, marriages and deaths were maintained by church parishes. Many were kept in Latin. In 1811 the church registers were surrendered to the local civil government. The majority of these registers have been filmed by the Church of Jesus Christ of Latter-Day Saints, so they are accessible through their family history centres or at the Centraal Bureau voor Genealogie (CBG) (Central Bureau for Genealogy) in The Hague. The Reformed churches also kept lists of members of their churches. Local civic authorities held marriage announcements and records of taxes levied on marriages and burials. Only marriages conducted by the Dutch Reformed Church were recognised so those outside it either had to be married in a Reformed church or by a civil service conducted by the local authority. Most of these records begin in the seventeenth century. The local authorities also maintained civil or gate books, comprising lists of those who gained the right to practise a trade or an occupation in a Dutch city; these were kept between the fifteenth to the nineteenth centuries. Local archives also hold documents like wills, property deeds and court records for both civil and criminal cases.

One of the major problems in using Dutch records is naming patterns. It was not until 1687 that the use of fixed surnames was introduced and this was not enforced in some provinces before 1811, when, under Napoleon's rule, all Dutch people were required to choose and use one surname. How far this applied to Huguenots, who arrived in the Netherlands with long-established surnames, is not established, but genealogists investigating their Dutch refugee ancestry need to be aware of this factor. Most Dutch people used patronymics. For men, the suffixes -se, -sen, or -szen were added to the father's name. The equivalent for daughters was -x or -dr. Diminutives were often used: Nicolas was shortened to Claes, so trying to find a Matthys Claessen would lead a researcher to look for his father Nicolas in marriage records. Alternatively, place names or occupations might be used. 'Van' means 'of' so 'van der Velde' means 'of the Field' and 'Smit' means 'Smith'. Sometimes nicknames referring to personal characteristics might be added: 'De Witt' means 'the white'. The same person could appear with a variety of names in different documents.

In 1945 the CBG was founded to give a central point where the public could access both national and private records relating to genealogy and heraldry. Its library has works on the history of many places in the Netherlands, periodicals and other family history-related publications. Among its holdings are copies of church records before and after 1811 and, perhaps of greatest importance to family historians seeking Protestant refugee ancestors, the Walloon Card Index. This consists of some 1.2 million references from Walloon churches in the Netherlands, Germany, France, the territories occupied by present-day Belgium and England between 1685 and 1811. This provides a useful single source to track migrant families across Europe. The CBG also holds files on families which have already been researched. The originals of the registers and other documents are in other national and regional archives, and the CBG staff can give advice on where to go for records they do not hold.

The Dutch Nationaal Archief (National Archive) is also in The Hague. It holds records of the central government, including what are called Military Books, in which people were registered by company. The National Archives are also the local record office for the ancient County of Holland. There is also material from private institutions, including the Dutch East India Company from 1602 to 1811.

Belgium

Created in 1830, Belgium is composed of a number of the ancient provinces of the Spanish Netherlands. It is still divided into Walloons and Flemings.

The French-speaking Walloon region accounts for about one-third of the population of Belgium. It consists of the provinces of Brabant, Namur, Hainaut, Liège and Luxembourg (not to be confused with the country of Luxembourg)

There is one main repository to help family historians tracing ancestors from the Spanish-ruled Low Countries, the Bibliothèque Wallonne (Walloon Library). John Peters's account (*A Family in Flanders*) of how he traced his family history in France, Belgium and Britain is a good introduction to sources in Belgium.

Géniwal (Généalogie Informatique Wallonie) has produced databases for those tracing their Walloon ancestors. Marriages in Wallonia, Belgium, 1559–1934 are on www.ancestry.com and there is an index of births, marriages and deaths from Wallonia on a CD-ROM.

Germany

A few of the first wave of Protestant refugees in the late sixteenth century came to the German states directly from France, especially from the eastern provinces, while others arrived from the Netherlands. They founded some Walloon settlements, such as those in Frankenthal, Mannheim, Heidelberg and Hanau, but families later moved from there into the Uckermark in the north-eastern part of Brandenburg-Prussia.

During the Thirty Years War (1618–48) little attention was paid to preserving official and church records and, of course, during this period, no refugees sought shelter in Germany – rather people fled from the country. In the 1680s, some 40,000 Huguenots migrated from France to Germany, welcomed in a number of states for their ability to help rebuild the economy after the Thirty Years War. The main places of Huguenot settlement were Brandenburg-Prussia, Hesse-Cassel, the Rhine-Main region, Franconia and the Palatinate. Some can barely have arrived in the Palatinate before the outbreak of war following the French king Louis XIV's invasion of the region in 1688, which lasted until 1697. It was another devastating episode: whole settlements were destroyed and burned to the ground and the Palatinate Huguenots fled again. In 1689 the Walloon congregation of Mannheim decamped as a body to Magdeburg in Saxony, but some sought refuge elsewhere. In 1703, for example, Judic Canonge,

The French church in Berlin

born in Mannheim, was summoned before the authorities of the Church of the Artillery in London to be rebuked for his scandalous behaviour (unfortunately not detailed). Dominique Guillemenot-Ehrmantraut has detailed the Mannheim church's history in *L'Église réformée de la langue française de Mannheim de 1652 à 1689* (The French-language Reformed church of Mannheim from 1652 to 1689). Other refugees from this war went to the Uckermark, others to Hesse, and some emigrated to America.

Brandenburg-Prussia

The prime destination for Huguenot refugees from France in the second wave of the seventeenth century was Brandenburg-Prussia, where some 20,000 refugees, about half of those who fled France for Germany, relocated. They were encouraged to come partly because of their skills and partly to rebuild the population, which had been devastated by the Thirty Years War. In Berlin they remained a united community, building a splendid church, the French Cathedral, which was modelled on a destroyed Huguenot church in Charenton-Saint-Maurice in France. They preserved their language until 1806, when they decided to conduct services in German to show their opposition to Napoleon's occupation of Prussia. There were other communities in Brandenburg and Potsdam to the south of Berlin. Smaller settlements were in Alt Landsberg, Angermuende, Battin, Bergolz, Bernau, Braunsberg, Buchholz, Cottbus,

A card, advertising meat extract, shows Huguenots being welcomed into Berlin

109

Eberswalde, Frankfurt-am-Oder, Gramzow, Gross-Ziethen, Hammel-spring, Koepenick, Lonow, Melzow, Muencheberg, Neuruppin, Neustadt-an-der-Dosse, Oranienburg, Parstein, Potzlow, Prenzlau, Schmargendorf, Schwedt, Spandau, Storbeck and Strasburg (not to be confused with Strasbourg in Alsace, France). Later economic problems in the Uckemark led to Huguenots re-emigrating, going to Pomerania, East Prussia and Denmark, while others went into the army.

Hessen

Roughly 3,500 refugees went to Hesse-Cassel. Many Huguenot refugees passed through Frankfurt-am-Main, and a number settled in the town of Cassel and the area north of it. A Huguenot town, Neu-Isenburg, was created near Frankfurt in 1699. The town of Bad Karlshafen was also specifically established for Huguenots and today there is a museum there.

Lower Saxony (Niedersachsen)

Some 1,200 Huguenots migrated to Hanover and the surrounding area. The town of Hanover itself, where some 250 went, was Lutheran but a

The German Huguenot Museum in Bad Karlshafen is housed in an old cigar factory.

Inside the museum are recreations of the kind of homes the Huguenots would have known.

Calvinist French congregation was established in 1690. George, the Elector of Hanover, succeeded to the British throne in 1714 as George I. His wife, Sophia Dorothea of Celle, was the daughter of a Huguenot duchess and there were a number of her compatriots in her employ. She had been brought up as a Calvinist. Huguenot refugees are first mentioned in Celle in 1665 and established a church there in 1686. After his accession to the British throne, George I remained the ruler of Hanover, and a number of Huguenots and their descendants travelled between the two countries, both before and after his accession. The Huguenot community in Hanover, however, did not long survive the second generation, which suggests they either assimilated or migrated to other communities.

At the end of the seventeenth century, the nearby town of Hamelin had some 500–600 Huguenots, mainly employed in manufacturing industries. This community dwindled over the next half-century: by 1754 there were just 159.

Other Huguenot churches were established in Leipzig, Celle, Erlangen, Schwabach near Nuremberg, Halle and Stuttgart. There was also a community in Strasbourg, now in France.

Baveria (Bayern)

The main settlement of Huguenots in this region was in the north, in an area called Franconia. A Huguenot church was built in the town of Schwabach in 1687.

Modern German states

1	Schleswig-Holstein	10	Hessen
2	Mecklenburg-Western Pomerania	11	Thuringia
3	Hamburg (City State)	12	Saxony
4	Lower Saxony	13	Rheinland-Palatinate
5	Bremen (City State)	14	Saarland
6	Berlin (City State)	15	Bavaria
7	Saxony-Anhalt	16	Baden-Wurttemberg
8	Brandenburg	17	Hollenzollern
9	North Rhein-Westphalia		

Saarland

An early French Protestant community was established in the Saarland in 1604, mainly around a glassworks, in order to bring trade to the area. Other migrants worked in textiles. There is still an active congregation here, including some descendants of the original settlers, but a number of members emigrated to the United States in the 1890s.

Researching ancestors in Germany

Old handwriting is always a problem to decipher, but in German there is an additional factor. Until the twentieth century a Gothic style, called 'black letter', was used for both printed and handwritten material. Although print is not too difficult to read, it is impossible to decipher some handwriting without considerable practice, even for German-speakers, in the same way that reading older English documents in secretary hand needs specialist knowledge.

Your ancestors may have assimilated into the general population, so their baptisms, marriages and burials will be entered in local churches. Many of these parish registers remain with the original church. The Anglo-German Family History Society publishes various guides to researching German ancestors.

The records in Germany are kept locally, each state having its own archives.

Switzerland

Switzerland was, and still is, divided into twenty-five self-governing cantons, which were not formed into a confederation until 1848. The country has four official languages: French, German, Italian and Romansch.

The Swiss theological reformer Ulrich Zwingli (1484–1531) effectively converted French-speaking Geneva to the Reformed religion. After Jean Calvin had travelled around Europe, he finally settled in Geneva, where he was extremely influential. With the enthusiastic support of the authorities, he established what they regarded as a model church and community. Geneva became a magnet for those who followed what they regarded as a purer form of Protestantism and also for ministers studying theology. Some pastors came from studying there to serve in England, such as Jean Dubourdieu.

The predominantly Protestant cantons were mostly German-speaking: Appenzell-Ausserrhoden, Basel (where both French and German were spoken), Bern, Genf/Geneva (French-speaking), Neuchâtel (French-speaking), Schaffhausen, Vaud and Zürich. Mixed Roman Catholic and

Protestant were Aargau (mainly Protestant), Glarus, Graubünden, Sankt Gallen, and Thurgau (mainly Protestant). The rest were predominantly Catholic and unlikely to contain Protestants, either native-born or migrants from elsewhere.

A number of people from the Swiss cantons, especially Vaud, can be found in the French church registers in London and a handful in congregations outside the capital. The relatively few Italians who converted to Protestantism seem to have migrated to Switzerland. From there some moved on, such as Nicollas Ciangolo, a Sicilian, who brought an attestation from Geneva to St Jean, Spitalfields and was admitted into the church on 15 September 1717. Others, such as Jean Descuq, came from the village of St Paul de Lamiate in the Languedoc in France via Switzerland. He presented a certificate of his faith from Geneva to the authorities of St Jean, Spitalfields on 26 October 1718. Marcellin Girardet from Neuchâtel presented his attestation from 'Conigsberg' to the Threadneedle Street church in 1751. There is a town called Königsberg in Germany and a Kongsberg in the Netherlands, either of which might have been on his journey from Switzerland to London but there are other possible places with a similar name. There was a substantial Huguenot community in Neuchâtel: the Huguenot Library has a computer print-out of refugees who went there from France following the Revocation, which gives their places of origin, and Girardet may have been of this community.

Tracing ancestors in Switzerland

Because the different cantons are effectively self-governing, they all have their own archives and practices on what records were kept; where they are now deposited may vary from canton to canton. Although from the 1874 constitution basic rules for civil government have been set by the Confederation, this is after the period of Huguenot migration.

In Switzerland there is no central repository for archives, each canton keeping its own records. Civil registration was introduced in 1876. Before that, as in other places, church registers are the primary source of information. In some cantons parish registers have been deposited in the archives: in others they remain in the churches. It is essential to know at least the canton and ideally the district where your ancestors lived. Most Kantonsarchiv (state archives) will have at least microfilms of all church records still in existence in their canton, as well as the usual civil legal records.

There are some published family biographies. The following have been filmed or put on microfiche by the Church of Latter-Day Saints and can be consulted through their Family History Centers. The *Historisch-Biographisches Lexikon der Schweiz* (Historical-Biographical Dictionary of Switzerland) contains accounts of larger families, with more details on important members. The *Schweizerisches Geschlechterbuch* (Swiss Familybook) concentrates on the more famous families. Julius Billeter (1869–1957) made a collection of family histories, some dating back to the sixteenth century. Like all secondary sources, the information should be verified from the originals, but it will show where to start looking. A collection of information on families in Basel was made by Dr A. Lotz. In addition, there is a publication by Mario van Moos, *Bibliography of Swiss Genealogies*, which contains all known Swiss genealogies, both published and in archives. This has not been filmed but may be available through the Church of Latter-Day Saints or in specialist libraries.

Scandinavia

Approximately 2,000 religious refugees went to Denmark and the Nordic countries, which had embraced Lutheranism. Huguenots, however, were overwhelmingly Calvinists and Denmark refused to accept those who were driven out of England in 1553 when the Catholic Mary I succeeded her Protestant brother. In 1569 Denmark passed legislation which required all strangers wanting to settle in the country to swear an oath to Lutheran principles. In the French Church records, there are a few individuals from Denmark, such as Augustin Grimpie, who presented an attestation from the congregation at Copenhagen to the Threadneedle Street church in 1689. His birthplace is not given, so it is not known whether he was born in Copenhagen, or had simply stayed there for a few years after fleeing from France.

Sweden did not gain independence from Danish rule until 1520. The dismantling of the Catholic Church's power there began in 1527 and the Reformation took root in 1536, but conflict between Lutherans and Calvinists continued for many years. Calvinists were granted toleration, so long as they did not cause trouble. The first migrants were mainly Dutch and were invited to Sweden, as they were to many other countries, in order to bring economic benefit, and some occupied important posts at court. They were not recruited for their skills in textile manufacture but for their commercial experience and metal-working skills. It is estimated that some 5,000 French-speaking migrants, Walloons from both the Netherlands and from France, arrived in the early seventeenth century. Most settled in the capital, Stockholm, and some re-migrated. Isaac Grinpret, a young man, presented a certificate from his church in Stockholm to the Threadneedle Street church in 1711. Swedish church records 1500–1937 are now online at www.ancestry.com.

Chapter 7

SETTLEMENTS ELSEWHERE

The Americas

It is estimated that in the period before and after the Revocation of the Edict of Nantes between 10,000 and 15,000 Huguenots went to the Americas though there had also been previous efforts to set up communities there. The first was in Brazil in 1555, but five years later the 500 or so people who went there from France were overwhelmed by the Portuguese, who had begun to colonise the country in 1530. Thereafter Dutch and French Protestant refugees confined themselves to North America, which from the late sixteenth century was a destination for people who wished to escape religious discrimination or persecution in their homelands. To a lesser extent, they also relocated to the West Indies.

The United States

From the late sixteenth century the area of North America that became the United States was a destination for people who wished to escape religious discrimination or persecution in their homelands and most were Protestants, although there were some Catholic settlements.

By the time Huguenot emigration from France ceased around the middle of the eighteenth century, only the thirteen colonies on the eastern seaboard of North America were ruled by Britain. Florida and the western part of the landmass were controlled by Catholic Spain, which did not surrender its interests there until the nineteenth century. As territories were opened up to European settlers, Huguenots and their descendants moved into them. Georgia, for example, was founded in 1732 and in the following years some Huguenots moved there from Carolina, or purchased land there from absentee plantation owners. The expansion into the Mid-West and West Coast that took place in the nineteenth century brought hundreds of thousands of immigrants from Europe, many of whom had Huguenot ancestry, although they were no longer part of specific congregations there. The sheer number of immigrants attracted to the United States over the centuries means that many are likely to be of

Huguenot descent, even if they had lost knowledge of their French or Dutch roots by the time they arrived.

Following the American War of Independence (1775–83), many of those who remained loyal to the British Crown relocated to Canada, Britain or the West Indies, and among those who did there are likely to be at least some of Huguenot origin.

In 1710 an Act 'for Naturalizing such foreign Protestants and others therein mentioned, as are settled, or shall settle, in any of his Majesty's Colonies in America' was passed. The aim was to make the naturalisation of religious refugees simpler than the long and expensive process of obtaining a private Act. Those who had lived for seven years in any of the American colonies (which then included the West Indies) could take the prescribed oaths before the Chief Judge or indeed any judge of the colony where they lived. Very few, it must be admitted, took advantage of this legislation. Some preferred to obtain naturalisation through the various local colonial assemblies. Returns of naturalisations under this Act were made to the British government and have been published by the Huguenot Society (HSQS, Vol. XXIV, also on CD-ROM). Places of residence and, often, religion are given in these returns, which finish in 1768. All the returns were transcribed, not just those who are stated, or from their names appear, to be of French or Dutch origin.

New England

New England was a major destination in the Americas for those escaping religious persecution and they included emigrants from France and the Netherlands, who landed in Massachusetts, Connecticut, Delaware and New York. Thereafter the trade between England and the Netherlands, the mother countries, and their American colonies led to many links with Huguenots, including those who remained based in Europe. Some of these earlier traders did not settle permanently in America, but returned to Europe having made money.

In 1685 a specifically French church was established in Boston, Massachusetts, which remained until 1748, by which time the Huguenots were assimilated into the general population of the town. Technically only Congregationalists were allowed to vote at that time, although it seems that exceptions were made for some Huguenots.

New York

New York was originally settled by the Dutch, who called it New Amsterdam. The name was changed when the British took it over in 1664. The first Dutch congregation here was established in 1628. Many of its members, however, were people of French origin who had fled to the Netherlands in the first period of persecution in the sixteenth century. The French Walloon and Dutch Reformed shared a church building, although

117

they conducted services in their own languages. It became known as L'Église française à la Nouvelle-Amsterdam (the French Church at New Amsterdam). Initially nonconformist, it closed in 1776 and reopened in 1796 when its congregation voted to become Episcopalian, the equivalent of the Anglican Church in England. Weekly services in French are still held in the church on East 61st Street.

Huguenots also went to predominantly Dutch Staten Island and founded a church there in the early 1660s; only its graveyard remains. The arrival of more refugees swelled the congregation to the point where another building had to be used. This was before either the Dutch or the English had their own churches. This congregation lasted until the mid-eighteenth century and eventually merged with the Dutch Reformed church there. Luckily the minister at the time was fluent in both French and Dutch.

Huguenot migrants moved into the surrounding countryside, going to Ulster County to the town of Kingston, then primarily a Dutch settlement, and later purchasing land nearby to create New Paltz, where the first church in this region was built in 1678. A few of their houses still survive in Huguenot Street, perhaps the oldest street in the United States.

Around the period of the dragonnades and the Revocation of the Edict of Nantes, another group of refugees, from France via England, arrived in New York. Around 1689 many settled in New Rochelle, which was named to commemorate the town of La Rochelle in France, a major stronghold of

The Huguenot Memorial at New Rochelle in New York

Protestantism which had endured an eighteen-month siege by the king's troops in 1626–8. Later they were joined by some who had initially fled to the West Indies but moved on. Their church was erected sometime after 1691.

A settlement at Narragansett on Rhode Island was organised in London and a group of migrants arrived in 1686. Unfortunately they did not have title to the land and were driven off in 1691.

Florida

In 1564 a Protestant town was founded at Fort Caroline, near present-day Jacksonville in Florida, then a Spanish possession. A year later the inhabitants were attacked by the Spanish and the few survivors returned to their homelands in France and Wales. A later attempt to found a Huguenot settlement in 1766 at Campbell Town also foundered after a couple of years. Where the families that had originally settled here went after the dissolution of their communities is not yet known.

Virginia

In 1630 a group of Huguenots aiming for South Carolina were offloaded on the James River at Virginia. What happened to them is unknown – no records have survived but later official records do contain names of French origin. In 1700 another project sponsored by William III of England resulted in five shiploads of Huguenot migrants, led by the French Huguenot Charles de Sailly (from Ireland), arriving. They were largely second- or third-generation French people, descended from refugees in different parts of Europe. Some were from the Swiss cantons, where French and Italian Protestants had taken shelter. Others seem to have been from Ireland and were being rewarded for military successes. They also settled on the James River in what was called Manakin Town, after the Native Americans from whom the land had been purchased.

South Carolina

In 1562 the French Protestant war hero Gaspard de Coligny, (who was later the primary target of the Massacre of St Bartholomew), created the first Huguenot settlement in North America. Thirty families were established at Port Royal, near what became Charleston in South Carolina.

By 1700 about 450 Huguenots from France had settled in South Carolina and founded a church in Charlestown (later Charleston) around 1681. The first building on its present site in Church Street was constructed in 1687 but was destroyed in 1796 to stop the spread of a fire in the town. The replacement was succeeded by a new building in the then-fashionable Gothic style, which opened in 1845. Services were conducted in French until 1828 and today it still uses a translated adaptation of the liturgy of the churches of Neuchâtel and Vallangin, with additions from the

The Huguenot church in Charleston, South Carolina

Protestant Episcopal Church. It is now the only remaining independent Huguenot church in America.

Other Huguenot settlements established in and after the 1680s were at Goose Creek in Berkeley County across the bay from Charleston; Orange Quarter, also in Berkeley County; French Santee, forty miles north of Charleston in Craven County, and St John's Barclay to the west of Goose Creek. One of the waterways flowing into the Cooper River became known as French Creek. The name of the settlement at New Bordeaux (established in 1765) suggests the origin of its first inhabitants. The founder of the town of Purysburg (1732) was Jean Pierre Purry from Neuchâtel in Switzerland. Purysburg is generally regarded as a Huguenot settlement but the original inhabitants were Swiss Protestants, most of whom were French-speaking.

Canada

The eastern provinces of the part of North America which became Canada were initially settled by both British and French emigrants. The western part of the landmass was not settled by Europeans until the nineteenth century, although there were fur trappers living there and traders with the native Canadians, especially around Hudson Bay, where the British Hudson Bay Company operated. France claimed the whole of the country but ceded sovereignty to Britain in 1713.

It was not until 1598 that any permanent settlement in Canada was created by the French and this was in Nova Scotia, where the Huguenot Pierre du Gast founded Port Royal. Further French communities were set up in other territories and many who went there were apparently Huguenots. A Catholic missionary drive from 1610, after Henri IV of France, who was sympathetic to Protestantism, was assassinated, forced many Huguenots to relocate to the Dutch settlement on Manhattan Island. Until the War of Independence (1775–83) the whole of North America was ruled by Britain. Canada chose to remain under British sovereignty at the end of the war and some of Huguenot descent in the American states relocated there.

The twelve provinces and territories of Canada each holds its own records. The records of the Hudson Bay Company are held in the University of Manitoba.

West Indies

The Caribbean islands were of vital importance to the European powers that settled them, both for their location and for the economic profits from the crops produced there, mainly sugar but also rum, tobacco and indigo. The French islands had some Huguenot settlers but after the Revocation of the Edict of Nantes they had to leave if they wanted to retain their religion. Most, like David de Bonrepos, pastor of the Calvinist church on St Kitts, relocated to North America. He and his brother initially went to Boston but then to the settlement at New Rochelle.

Because it was a destination that promised riches, people of Huguenot origin went to the British colonies there. They did not establish separate Huguenot communities or churches so records relating to those of French and Dutch ancestry who went there will be found in the standard record sources.

Following the American War of Independence, many of those who remained loyal to the British Crown also relocated to the West Indies and among those who did there are likely to be at least some of Huguenot origin.

South Africa

Another Huguenot destination was South Africa. In 1650 the Dutch established a permanent settlement at the Cape of Good Hope, where both they and the English had been stopping off on their way to their possessions in Asia. Between 1670 and 1700, a number of refugees who had fled to the Netherlands were encouraged to relocate to South Africa. There were only about 200, but they had superior skills so became highly influential in the new colony. They were given land in different locations but the majority settled in Hoek, near Stellenbosch, and Drakenstein. Some were of French origin and there was tension between them and the Dutch settlers. A village that developed around two farms, La Cotte and Cabriere, marked the beginnings of Franschhoek, which means 'French corner'. There is now a museum and a memorial here. In the seventeenth and eighteenth centuries, only the Dutch Reformed Church was officially recognised so the French element was assimilated and their descendants today speak Afrikaans.

Australia

Australia, like other members of the former British Empire, has descendants of Huguenot ancestry among its population, although they did not establish separate churches. The first arrivals were mainly convicts – Huguenots committed crimes just like everyone else – but others are descended from people who emigrated there in search of a better life. Some

The Huguenot Memorial at Franschhoek

500 known Huguenot families have been detailed in *The Hidden Thread: Huguenot Families in Australia*, edited by Robert Nash.

The records relating to these and all the other countries to which Huguenots and their descendants went will be found in the standard records of the various places. There are family history societies and publications to help researchers in their quest to find out about their brave, determined and resourceful forebears who left their countries to start new lives where they could practise the faith for which they were persecuted.

APPENDIX

Basic French and Dutch

Strictly speaking, Walloons spoke a dialect of French called Walcq and the Flemings spoke Flemish, closely related to Dutch. However, their churches were called the French and Dutch churches, so I have preserved this usage. To read the registers of either church, you need a basic vocabulary. Luckily they are written to a standard format but the French registers include more information than is generally found in English records, often involving details of relationships. Most register entries are heavily abbreviated. The following are the most commonly found:

French

Ane	=	*Ancien* (elder of the church)
Arch.	=	*Archevêque* (Archbishop)
Bap.	=	*Baptisé* (Baptised)
dud.	=	*dudit* (of the said, [singular])
desd.	=	*desdits* (of the said, [plural])
dem.	=	*demeurant* (living)
ég.	=	*église* (church)
f.	=	*fils* (son)
ff.	=	*fille* (daughter)
fem.	=	*femme* (wife)
lad.	=	*ladite* (the said, [female])
led.	=	*ledit* (the said, [male])
M.	=	*Marraine* (godmother)
Min.	=	*Ministre* (minister)
n.	=	*natif* (native)
P.	=	*Parrain* (godfather)
par.	=	*paroisse* (parish)
prov.	=	*province*
pub.	=	*publié* (published)
Sec.	=	*Secrétaire* (secretary)
sig.	=	*signé* (signed)
Sr.	=	*Sieur* (sir)
Tém.	=	*Témoin* (witness)

V./Vf.	=	*veuf* (widower)
Vve.	=	*veuve* (widow)

Other useful words and terms:

à	=	at/to
annonces	=	announcements (banns)
dans	–	in
par	=	by
de	=	of
épouse	=	spouse
feu	=	late
son/sa	=	his/her
promesse	=	promise (to marry)
né	=	born (masculine)
née	=	born (feminine)

Months

Jan.	=	*Janvier* (January)
Fev.	=	*Fevrier* (February)
Mars	=	March
Avr	=	*Avril* (April)
Mai	=	May
Juin	=	June
Juil.	=	*Juillet* (July)
Août	=	August
Séptembre	–	September
Octobre	=	October
Novembre	=	November
Décembre	=	December

The following examples come from London churches because they habitually included more information than those elsewhere.

From the church of Le Quarré:

1709 6 Mars. Ester, ff. de Mr Jean Suidre, apotiquaire, et de Dam. Marie Madeleine. Min. Mr Jounneau. P. Mr François Dubois, min. dem. à Islington. M. La mère pour Damelle Ester Lambert, sa sœur. Née 18 Fév.

(1709 6 March. Ester, daughter of Mr Jean Suidre, apothecary, and of Madame Marie Madeleine. Minister Mr Jounneau. Godfather Mr François Dubois, min[ister] living at Islington. Godmother the mother for Miss Ester Lambert, her sister [i.e. the child's aunt]. Born 18 Feb[ruary].)

From the Church of the Artillery marriage entries:

1735, 25 Dec. Jean Heraud, f. d'Abraham Heraud, et de Marie Clemenceau, de Vaux, en Saintonge—Madeleine Renaime, ff. de feu Jean Renaime, et de feue Marie Roy, de Maraine, en Saintonge ; mar. par Mr. Jacob Bourdillon, Min. de cette ég. Annonces publiées à l'ég. de la Patente ; Cert. Signé par Abraham David, Ane. et Sec., et par Balguerie de Chautard, Past. Téms. Abraham Heraud, Jaque Reneme, Pierre Mazell, Sec., Daniel de la Cour, Ane., Louis Desormeaux.

(1735, 25 Dec. Jean Heraud, son of Abraham Heraud, and of Marie Clemenceau, from Vaux, in Saintonge—Madeleine Renaime, daughter of the late Jean Renaime, and the late Marie Roy, from Maraine, in Saintonge; mar[ried] by Mr. Jacob Bourdillon, Min[ister] of this ch[urch]. Banns published at the ch[urch] of La Patente ; Cert[ificate] signed by Abraham David, Elder and Sec[retary] and by Balguerie de Chautard, Past[or]. Wit[nesses]. Abraham Heraud, Jaque Reneme, Pierre Mazell, Sec[retary], Daniel de la Cour, Elder, Louis Desormeaux.)

Dutch

Because Dutch and English are so similar, even non-Dutch readers can work out the salient points of the following entries from the registers of the Dutch church in Colchester and realise that De Getuijgen (often abbreviated as Get) must mean 'the godparents'. Months of the year present no problems. This is the standard entry; there is less information given than in other churches.

1645 October 19 Ioanna, de doghter van Jan Behagel en Margriete. De Getuijgen, Claes Behagel, Gregorius Hennekens, en Maeijken vander Lende.

Eduard, s. van Abraham Hagedoorn en [blank]. Get. Eduard Colman, Samuel
Hagedoorn, en Sara Tayspil. Geb. den selven dag en was gedoopt bij Mr. Powel, pred. van Marys Parochie. Feb. 2.

The last sentence translates as 'born the same day and was baptised by Mr Powel, minister of Mary's Parish. Feb. 2'.

1690 Jacobus, s. van Nicolaus De Bruinne en Susanna. Get. Abraham de Bruijne, James Croket, s. van Josua, en Juffr. de Bruine d'oude. Geb. 20 Jan. en ged. in huvs. Jan. 30.

(1690 Jacobus, s[on] of Nicolas de Bruinne and Susanna. Godparents Abraham de Bruijne, James Croket, s[on] of Josua, and Juffr. de Bruine the elder. Born 20 Jan. and baptised in [their] house Jan. 30.)

Other useful words and phrases:

De oude	=	the older
De jonge	=	the younger
Geb.	=	*Geboren* (born)
Ged.	=	*Gedoopt* (baptised)
(Huys)vrouw	=	wife
in huys/huis	=	in house (i.e. baptised at home rather than in the church)

SELECTED BIBLIOGRAPHY

Unless otherwise stated, the place of publication is London.

Genealogical Research

There are numerous works on different aspects of genealogical research: the following is a selection.

Aldous, Vivienne E., *My Ancestors were Freemen of the City of London* (Society of Genealogists, 1999).

Chater, Kathy, *Tracing Your Family Tree in England, Ireland, Scotland and Wales* (Lorenz Books, 2nd ed., 2009).

Costello, Vivian, *Researching Huguenot Settlers in Ireland*. This guide is available to download for free from the Brigham Young University's online family history journal: BYU Family Historian, Vol. 6 (Fall 2007), pp. 83–163 at www.lib.byu.edu/dlib/spc/famhistorian/index.html. Use the browse function to locate Vol. 6.

Gibson Guides, compiled by Jeremy Gibson (sometimes with another researcher) list county by county the surviving records and their location relating to a specific subject: marriage licences, coroners records, various taxes, poll books, electoral registers, local newspapers, militia lists, probate jurisdictions, victuallers' licences, etc. Early editions of these booklets were published by the Federation of Family History Societies and they are now produced by the Family History Partnership.

Hawkings, David T., *Criminal Ancestors: A Guide to Historical Criminal Records in England and Wales* (The History Press, Stroud, 2nd ed., 2009).

Herber, Mark, *Ancestral Trails* (Softback Preview, 2nd ed., 2004).

Scottish Record Office, *Tracing Your Scottish Ancestors: The Official Guide* (Birlinn Limited, 2007).

Sinclair, Cecil, *Tracing Scottish Local History* (HMSO, Edinburgh, 1994).

Wade, Stephen, *Tracing Your Criminal Ancestors* (Pen & Sword, 2009)

Huguenots

Huguenot Society Quarto Series (HSQS), published by the Huguenot Society of Great Britain and Ireland

Volume	Title
I	The Walloons and their Church at Norwich, their History and Register, 1565–1832.
II	Les Actes des Colloques des Eglises françaises et des Synodes des Églises Étrangères réfugiées en Angleterre, 1581–1654.
III	Register of the Protestant Church at Guisnes, 1668–1685.
IV	Registre de l'Église Wallonne de Southampton [1567–1779].
V	Registers of the Walloon Church in Canterbury, Parts 1–3 [1581–1837].
VI	Despatches of Michele Suriano and Marc'Antonio Barbaro, Venetian Ambassadors at the Court of France, 1560–1563.
VII	Registers of the French Conformed Churches at St Patrick and St Mary, Dublin [1668–1830].
VIII	Letters of Denization and Acts of Naturalization for Aliens in England, 1509–1603.
IX	Registers of the French Church of Threadneedle Street, London, Part I [1600–1636].
X	Lists of Aliens Resident in London, Henry VIII to James I, Parts I, II and III and Index.
XI	Register of the French Church of La Patente, Spitalfields, London, 1689–1785.
XII	Register of the Dutch Church, Colchester [1645–1728].
XIII	Register of the French Church of Threadneedle Street, London, Part II [1636–1694].
XIV	Registers of the French Nonconformist Churches, Dublin [1701–1731 and 1771–1831].
XV	History of the Walloon and Huguenot Church at Canterbury.
XVI	Registers of the French Church of Threadneedle Street, London, Part III [1685–1714].
XVII	Register of the French Church, Thorney [1654–1738].
XVIII	Letters of Denization and Acts of Naturalization in England and Ireland, 1603–1700.
XIX	Register of the French Church, Portarlington, Ireland [1694–1816].
XX	Registers of the French Churches, Bristol [1687–1807], Plymouth [1733–1807], Stonehouse [1692–1791] and Thorpe-le-Soken [1684–1726].
XXI	Le Livre des Tesmoignages de l'Eglise de Threadneedle Street, 1669–1789.

XXII	Le Livre des Conversions et des Reconnoissances faites à l'Eglise française de la Savoye, 1684–1702.
XXIII	Register of the French Church of Threadneedle Street, London, Part IV [1707–1840].
XXIV	Lists of Naturalization of Foreign Protestants in the American Colonies under Stat. 13 Geo II.
XXV	Registers of the French Church of Le Carre and Berwick Street, London [1690–1788].
XXVI	Registers of the French Churches of the Savoy, Spring Gardens and Les Grecs, London [1684–1900].
XXVII	Letters of Denization and Acts of Naturalization in England and Ireland, 1701–1800.
XXVIII	Registers of the French Churches of the Chapel Royal, St James [1700–1756], and Swallow Street, London [1689–1709].
XXIX	Registers of the French Churches of the Tabernacle, Glasshouse Street [1696–1719], and Leicester Fields, London [1688–1783].
XXX	Registers of the French Church of Rider Court, London [1700–1747].
XXXI	Register of the French Church of Hungerford Market, later Castle Street, London [1688–1754].
XXXII	Registers of the French Churches of Le Petit Charenton [1701–1705], West Street [1706–1743], Pearl Street and Crispin Street [1694–1716], London.
XXXIII	Extracts from the Court Books of the Weavers' Company of London.
XXXIV	Mémoires inédits d'Abraham Mazel et d'Elie Marion sur la Guerre des Cévennes.
XXXV	A Supplement to Dr W.A. Shaw's Letters of Denization and Acts of Naturalization (Vols. XVIII and XXVII).
XXXVI	Register of the Walloon Church of Cadzand in Holland.
XXXVII	Register of the Church of St Martin Orgars with its history and that of the Swallow Street Church [1698–1762].
XXXVIII	Actes du Consistoire de l'Église Française de Threadneedle Street, London, Vol. I, 1560–1565.
XXXIX	Register of the French Church of Saint Jean, Spitalfields [1687–1761].
XL	Aufrère Letters and Papers.
XLI	Lists of Huguenot Pensioners in Ireland.
XLII	Register of the Artillery Church, London [1691–1786].
XLIII	Correspondence of Jacques Serces, Vol. I.
XLIV	Correspondence of Jacques Serces, Vol. II.
XLV	Registers of Wheeler Street [1703–1741], Swanfields [1721–1735], Hoxton [1751–1783], La Patente de Soho [1689–1782], Répertoire Général.

XLVI   A calendar of the correspondence of J. H. Ott, 1658–7.

XLVII   Registers of Le Mans.

XLVIII   Actes du Consistoire de l'Église Française de Threadneedle Street, London, Vol. II, 1571–77.

XLIX   Relief of French Protestant Refugees, 1681–87.

L   Archives of the French Protestant Church of London: a handlist.

LI   Records in the Huguenot Library: The Royal Bounty and connected Funds, The Burn Donation, The Savoy Church.

LII   French Protestant Hospital: inmates of, and applicants to, 1718–1957, and applicants for the Coqueau Charity 1745–1901, A–K.

LIII   French Protestant Hospital: inmates of, and applicants to, 1718–1957, and applicants for the Coqueau Charity 1745–1901, L–Z.

LIV   Calendar and Letter Books of the French Church of London, 1643–59.

LV   The case book of 'La Maison de Charité de Spitalflelds' 1739–41.

LVI   Catalogue of Remaining Manuscripts in the Huguenot Library.

LVII   Returns of strangers in the metropolis 1593, 1627, 1635, 1639.

LVIII   Minutes of the Consistory of the French Church of London, 1679–92.

LIX   Minutes of the Coetus of London, 1575–98 and Consistory Minutes of the Italian Church of London, 1570–91.

LX   Huguenot Wills and Administrations in England and Ireland 1617–1849, and Part 2, Complete Index of Names.

LXI   A Further Catalogue of Material Held in the Huguenot Library.

New Series

No 1   The Life and 'Mémoires Secrets' of Jean Des Champs, 1706–67.

No 2   Memoirs of the Reverend Jacques Fontaine, 1658–1728.

No 3   The French-speaking Reformed Community and their Church in Southampton, 1567–c. 1620.

No 4   Memoirs of Isaac Dumont de Bostaquet, 1632–1709, a gentleman of Normandy.

Indexes

General Index to Quarto Series and Proceedings (1986).
Supplementary Index to Proceedings (1991).
Master Index to Proceedings, Vols 1–26 (1998).

CD-ROM 1: Threadneedle Street Extracts
Vol. IX: Registers of the French Church of Threadneedle Street, London, Part I.

Vol. XIII: Register of the French Church of Threadneedle Street, London, Part II.

Vol. XVI: Registers of the French Church of Threadneedle Street, London, Part III.

Vol. XXIII: Register of the French Church of Threadneedle Street, London, Part IV.

CD-ROM 2: Spitalfields
Vol. XI: Register of the French Church of La Patente, Spitalfields, London.

Vol. XXXIX: Register of the French Church of Saint Jean, Spitalfields.

CD-ROM 3: (Double CD) Denization and Naturalisation
Vol. X: Lists of Aliens Resident in London, Henry VIII to James I, Parts I, II and III and Index.

Vol. LVII: Returns of strangers in the metropolis 1593, 1627, 1635, 1639.

Vol. VIII: Letters of Denization and Acts of Naturalization for Aliens in England, 1509–1603.

Vol. XVIII: Letters of Denization and Acts of Naturalization in England and Ireland, 1603–1700.

Vol. XXVII: Letters of Denization and Acts of Naturalization in England and Ireland, 1701–1800.

Vol. XXXV: A Supplement to Dr W. A. Shaw's Letters of Denization and Acts of Naturalization in Vols. XVIII and XXVII.

CD-ROM 3A: Naturalizations of Foreign Protestants in the Americas
Volume XXIV: Naturalizations of Foreign Protestants in the American and West India Colonies Pursuant to Statute 13 George II, c.7.

CD-ROM 4: Irish Extracts
Vol. VII: Registers of the French Conformed Churches at St Patrick and St Mary, Dublin.

Vol. XIV: Registers of the French Nonconformist Churches, Dublin.

Vol. XIX: Register of the French Church, Portarlington, Ireland.

Vol. XLI: Lists of Huguenot Pensioners in Ireland.

CD Rom 5A: Walloon and Huguenot churches outside London (1)
Vol. I: The Walloons and their Church at Norwich, their History and Register, 1565–1832, 1 vol. in 2 parts.

Vol. XII: Register of the Dutch Church, Colchester.

Vol. XVII: Register of the French Church, Thorney.

Vol. XX: Register of the French Church, Thorpe-le-Soken.

CD Rom 5 B: Walloon and Huguenot churches outside London (2)
Vol. IV: Registre de l'Eglise Wallonne de Southampton.
Vol. V: Registers of the Walloon Church in Canterbury, Parts 1–3.
Vol. XV: History of the Walloon and Huguenot Church at Canterbury.
Vol. XX: Registers of the French Churches, Bristol, Plymouth, and Stonehouse.

CD-ROM 6: Inmates of the French Hospital, 1745–1901
Vols. LII, LIII: French Protestant Hospital: inmates of, and applicants to, 1718–1957, and applicants for the Coqueau Charity 1745–1901.
Vol. LV: The Case Book of 'La Maison de Charité de Spittlefields' 1739–1741

CD-ROM 7: Huguenot Churches in London
Vol. XXV: Registers of the French Church of Le Carré and Berwick Street, London.
Vol. XXVI: Registers of the French Churches of the Savoy, Spring Gardens and les Grecs, London.
Vol. XXII: Le Livre des Conversions et des Reconnoissances faites à l'Eglise française de la Savoye, 1684–1702.
Vol. XXVIII: Registers of the French Churches of the Chapel Royal, St James, and Swallow Street, London.
Vol. XXIX: Registers of the French Churches of the Tabernacle, Glasshouse Street, and Leicester Fields, London.
Vol. XXX: Registers of the French Church of Rider Court, London.
Vol. XXXI: Register of the French Church of Hungerford Market, later Castle Street, London.
Vol. XXXII: Registers of the French Churches of Le Petit Charenton, West Street, Pearl Street, and Crispin Street, London.
Vol. XXXVII: Register of the Church of St Martin Orgars with its history and that of Swallow Street Church.
Vol. XLII: Register of the Artillery Church, London.
Vol. XLV: Registers of Wheeler Street, Swanfields, Hoxton, la Patente de Soho, Répertoire Général.

CD-ROM 8: Consistory and Administrative Records, c. 1560–1660
Volume II: Les Actes des Colloques des Eglises Françaises et des Synodes des Eglises Estrangers Refugiées en Angleterre, 1581–1654.
Volume XXXVIII: Actes du Consistoire de l'Eglise Française de Threadneedle Street, Londres, Vol. I, 1560–1565.
Volume XLVIII: Actes du Consistoire de l'Eglise Française de Threadneedle Street, Londres, Vol. II, 1571–1577.
Volume LIV: A Calendar of the Letter Books of the French Church of London from the Civil War to the Restoration, 1643–1659.

Volume LIX: Unity in Conformity: The Minutes of the Coetus of London, 1575 and the Consistory Minutes of the Italian Church of London, 1570–1591

CD-ROM 9: Threadneedle Street and French Protestant Refugees, c. 1660–1700
Volume XXI: Le livre des Tesmoignages de l'Eglise de Threadneedle Street, 1669–1789.
Volume XLIX: French Protestant Refugees Relieved through the Threadneedle Street Church, London, 1681–1687.
Volume LVIII: Minutes of the Consistory of the French Church of London, Threadneedle Street, 1679–1692.

CD-ROM 10: Registers of the French Churches of Guines, Caszand, Dover and Le Mans
Volume III: Register of the Protestant Church at Guines, 1668–1685.
Volume XXXVI: Register of the Walloon Church at Cadzand in Holland
Volume XLVII: Registers of Le Mans.
Registers of the French Church at Dover, Kent (privately printed in 1888 by F.A. Crisp).

Huguenot Families: all twenty editions are now available on a single CD-ROM from the Huguenot Society.

Other publications containing records of Dutch and Huguenot churches:

Crisp, F.A., *Registers of the French Church at Dover, Kent* (privately printed 1888).
Hessels, J.H. (ed./trans.), *Register of the Attestations or Certificates of Membership, Confessions of Guilt, Certificates of Marriages, Betrothals, Publications of Banns, &c, &c. Preserved in the Dutch Reformed Church, Austin Friars, London, 1568 to 1872* (London, Consistory of the Dutch Church, 1892).
Kretschmar, F.G.L.O., *De registers van de 'Dutch Chapel Royal' 1694–1775* (Jaarboek Central Bureau Voor Genealogie, Amsterdam, 1964).
Moens, W.J.C., *The marriage, baptismal and burial registers . . . of the Dutch Reformed Church, Austin Friars* (1884). Reissued by Archive CD Books (2004) as *London Dutch Church Register: Marriages, Confessions, Membership and Banns 1568–1872*.
Schelven, A.A. van, *Kerkeraads-protocollen der Nederduitsche vluchtellingen-kerk te London* (Amsterdam, 1923).

Nonconformist denominations

Breed, Geoffrey R., *My Ancestors Were Baptists* (Society of Genealogists, 1986).

Clifford, David J.H., *My Ancestors Were Congregationalists* (Society of Genealogists, 1997).

Leary, William, *My Ancestors Were Methodists* (Society of Genealogists, 1982, reprinted 1993).

Ruston, Alan, *My Ancestors Were English Presbyterians/Unitarians* (Society of Genealogists, 1993).

Steel, D.J., *Sources for Nonconformist Genealogy and Family History* (Phillimore for the Society of Genealogists, 1973).

General works

The following books will probably not, unless you are very lucky, mention your ancestors, but they will give background information about Huguenots in general.

Cottret, Bernard, *The Huguenots in England: Immigration and settlement c. 1550–1700* (CUP, Cambridge, 1985), translated by Peregrine Stevenson, originally published as *Terre d'Exile* (Aubier, Paris, 1985).

Currer-Briggs, Noel and Gambier, Royston, *Huguenot Ancestry* (Phillimore, 1985).

Gwynn, Robin D., *Huguenot Heritage: The history and contribution of the Huguenots in Britain* (Routledge, 1985).

Heal, Ambrose (Sir), *London Furniture Makers 1660–1840* (Portman Books, 1953; second edn, 1988)

Herber, Mark, *Clandestine Marriages in the Chapel and Rules of the Fleet Prison 1680-1754*, 3 vols (Francis Boutle, London, 1991–2000)

Hylton, Raymond, *Ireland's Huguenots and their Refuge, 1662–1745: An Unlikely Haven* (Sussex Academic Press, 2005).

Mayo, Ronald, *The Huguenots in Bristol* (Bristol, 1985), booklet published by the Bristol branch of the Historical Association.

Murdoch, Tessa and Vigne, Randolph, *The French Hospital in England: Its Huguenot History and Collections* (John Adamson, Cambridge, 2009).

Reaman, George Elmore, *The Trail of the Huguenots in Europe, the United States, South Africa and Canada* (Genealogical Publishing Co., 1963, reprinted 2000, with addenda and corrigenda by Milton Rubincam).

Schwartz, Hillel, *The French Prophets: The History of a Millenarian Group in Eighteenth-Century England* (University of California Press, Berkeley, 1980).

Scouladi, Irene (ed.), *Huguenots in Britain and their French Background* (Macmillan, 1987).

Vigne, Randolph and Littleton, Charles (eds.), *From Strangers to Citizens: The integration of immigrant communities in Britain, Ireland and Colonial America 1550–1750* (The Huguenot Society of Great Britain and Ireland/Sussex Academic Press, 2001).

The Spitalfields project (Council for British Archaeology) details the results of the excavation of the crypt of Christchurch, Spitalfields, between 1984 and 1986, where many people from Huguenot families were interred. The first two publications are scholarly accounts of the findings and the third a more accessible summary for the lay reader.

Reeve, Jez and Adams, Max, *Vol. 1: The Archaeology: Across the Styx* (CBA, York, 1993).
Molleson, Theya and Cox, Margaret with Waldron, A.H. and Whittaker, D.K., *Vol. 2: The Anthropology: the Middling Sort* (CBA, York, 1993).
Cox, Margaret, *Life and Death in Spitalfields 1700–1850* (CBA, York, 1996).

Overseas

Bernard, Gildas, *Les familles protestantes en France: XVIe siècle–1792: Guide des recherches biographiques et généalogiques* (Protestant Families in France: 18th century–1792: Guide to bibliographic and genealogical research) (Archives Nationales, Paris, 1987).
Carlo, Paula Wheeler, *Huguenot Refugees in Colonial New York* (Sussex Academic Press, Brighton, 2005).
Guillaume, H.M., Meyjes, Posthumus and Bots, Hans (eds. with the collaboration of Johanna Roelevink), *Livre des Actes des Églises Wallonnes aux Pays-Bas 1601–1697* (Book of the Acts of the Walloon Churches in the Netherlands 1601–1697) (Instituut voor Nederandse Geschiedenis, The Hague, 2005).
Historisch-Biographisches Lexikon der Schweiz (Historical-Biographical Dictionary of Switzerland) 7 vols (Neuenburg, 1921–34).
La Vie Protestante (The Protestant Life) is a series of books, fifty-two in total up to 2009, published in Paris, which concentrates on Protestantism in France, but also includes some volumes on overseas congregations in Britain, the Netherlands, Germany and the United States.
Moos, Mario van, *Bibliography of Swiss Genealogies*, 2 vols (Picton Press, Camden, ME, 1993).
Nash, Robert (ed.), *The Hidden Thread: Huguenot Families in Australia* (Huguenot Society of Australia, Newtown, NSW, 2010).
Peters, John, *A Family from Flanders* (Collins, 1985). This account of how the author traced his family is a good introduction to research in Belgium, France and Britain.

Zwicky, J.P., *Schweizerisches Geschlechterbuch* (Swiss Familybook) (Lendorff, Basel, 1905–25).

Academic journals

Most of these are of interest to academic historians or theologians working on Protestantism, but they also include some articles of use to genealogists, such as individuals' family histories or accounts of events in which their ancestors were involved. The Huguenot Library in London has copies.

Bulletin de la Société de l'Histoire du Protestantisme Français, 1853–present. Like the *Proceedings* of the HS, this has articles on a range of subjects from theological disputes to individuals' family history. It covers the entire history of Protestantism in France, not just the periods of oppression.
Bulletin de la Commission pour l'Histoire des Églises Wallonnes, 1877–1941.
Bulletin de la Société Vaudoise, later the *Bollettino della Società des Studi Valdesi*. Cultural and sociological studies of the religious minority from the medieval period to the modern day in the Swiss canton of Vaud.
Mémoires et Documents publiés par la Société d'Histoire et d'Archéologie de Genève, 1888–present.
Die Französiche Colonie, 1887–1900. Studies of the French Reformed communities in Germany.
Histoire de la Protestantism Belge, 1903–present.
Deutsche Hugenotten-Verein, later *Deutesche Hugenotton* and then *Hugenotten*, 1890–present.

Overseas Family History Societies Publications

All the Huguenot, Dutch and Walloon family history societies publish magazines and most send copies to the Huguenot Library in London. They may also produce other publications – check their websites.

ADDRESSES AND WEBSITES

Sources in Britain

Huguenots

The Huguenot Society
PO Box 3067
Warlingham
CR6 0AN
www.huguenotsociety.org.uk/

Huguenot Library Catalogue website http://library.ucl.ac.uk/F

For information on the Irish section, please contact by e-mail:
The Hon Secretary of the Irish Section <echohall@aol.com>

The Irish Huguenot Archive is housed in the RCB (Representative Church Body) Library:

RCB Library
Braemor Park
Dublin 14
Ireland
email: library@ireland.anglican.org

The Secretary
Huguenot and Walloon Research Association
Malmaison
Church Street
Great Bedwyn
Wiltshire
SN8 3PE

The Clerk
French Hospital
41 La Providence
Rochester

Kent
ME1 1NB
www.frenchhospital.org.uk
(This is the address for those wishing to enter or to visit the hospital. The records are in the Huguenot Library.)

There is as yet no museum dedicated to Huguenots in Britain but an appeal to create a National Huguenot Centre in Rochester, Kent, was launched in March 2011. It will be located at 95 High Street, close to La Providence.

Other Useful Addresses

Abney Park Cemetery
Abney Park Trust
South Lodge
Abney Park
Stoke Newington High Street
London
N16 0LH
www.abney-park.org.uk/

Access to Archives
www.nationalarchives.gov.uk/a2a/

Anglo-German Family History Society
www.afhs.org.uk

The Anglo-French Family History Society, for those of French but non-Huguenot ancestry, is not currently operating.

www.bmdregisters.co.uk has the digitised registers of miscellaneous Huguenot, nonconformist and other registers surrendered to the government in the nineteenth century and held in TNA.

Bristol Record Office
B Bond Warehouse
Smeaton Road
Bristol
BS1 6XN
www.bristol-city.gov.uk/recordoffice

Bristol & Avon Family History Society
www.bafhs.org.uk

Centre for Kentish Studies
Sessions House
County Hall
Maidstone
Kent
ME14 1XQ
www.kent.gov.uk/archives

Canterbury Cathedral Archives
The Precincts
Canterbury
CT1 2EH
www.canterbury-cathedral.org

City of London Cemetery and Crematorium
Aldersbrook Road
Manor Park
London
E12 5DQ
www.cityoflondon.gov.uk/Corporation/LGNL_Services/Community_
and_living/Deaths_funerals_and_cremations/Cemetery_and_
crematorium/

City of Westminster Archives Centre
10 St Ann's Street
London
SW1P 2DE
www.westminster.gov.uk

Church of Latter-day Saints/(International Genealogical Index) IGI
www.familysearch.org

Docklands Ancestor
www.parishregister.com

Dr Williams's Library
14 Gordon Square
London
WC1H 0AR
www.dwlib.co.uk/

Devon Record Office
Great Moor House
Bittern Road

Sowerton
Exeter,
Devon
EX2 7NL
www.devon.gov.uk/record_office

Dutch Church of London
7 Austin Friars
London EC2N 2HA
www.dutchchurch.org.uk

French Protestant Church of London
8–9 Soho Square
London
W1D 3QD
www.egliseprotestantelondres.org.uk

GOONS (Guild of One-Name Studies)
Box G
14 Charterhouse Buildings
Goswell Road
London
EC1M 7BA
www.one-name.org/

Guildhall Library
Aldermanbury
London
EC2P 2EJ
www.cityoflondon.ov.uk/Corporation/LGNL_services/Leisure_and_cu
lture/Libraries/City_of_London/libraries/guildhall_lib.htm

Hackney Archives
C.L.R. James Library
1–7 Beechwood Road
London
E8 3DG
www.hackney.gov.uk/ca-archives.htm

Institute of Historical Research Library
University of London
Senate House
Malet Street
London

WC1E 7HU
www.history.ac.uk/library

John Rylands University Library
150 Deansgate
Manchester
M4 3EH
www.library.manchester.ac.uk/Special Collections
Among the Library's Special Collections is the Methodist Archives and
Research Centre (MARC), which holds the Church's records. It also holds
the Christian Brethren Archive, a collection of material relating to assemblies of the Christians usually known as the Plymouth Brethren. This
movement began in Dublin, around 1827, and soon spread from Ireland to
Britain. The first English assembly was in Plymouth, and the movement
spread to Europe and the United States.

Kent Family History Society
www.kfhs.org.uk

Library of the Religious Society of Friends
Friends House
173–177 Euston Road
London
NW1 2BJ
www.quaker.org.uk/library

London Metropolitan Archives
40 Northampton Road
Clerkenwell
London
EC1R 0HB
www.cityoflondon.gov.uk/lma

Moravian Church
5 Muswell Hill
London
N10 3TJ

The National Archives
Ruskin Avenue
Kew
Richmond
Surrey
TW9 4DU

www.nationalarchives.gov.uk

National Register of Archives
www.nationalarchives.gov.uk/nra/

Norfolk Family History Society
www.norfolkfhs.org.uk

Norfolk Record Office
The Archive Centre
Martineau Lane
Norwich
NR1 2DQ
www.archives.norfolk.gov.uk

oldbaileyonline 1674–1913
www.oldbaileyonline.org

Parish Chest
www.parishchest.com
This company sells CD-ROMs and books on aspects of family history research, many, such as church register transcripts, produced by family history societies.

Random Acts of Genealogical Kindness
www.raogk.org/

Registry of Friendly Societies
www.mutuals.fsa.gov.uk/

S&N British Data Archive Ltd and S&N Genealogy Supplies
West Wing
Manor Farm
Chilmark
Salisbury
SP3 5AF
www.genealogysupplies.com/

Society of Genealogists
14 Charterhouse Buildings
London
EC1M 7BA
www.sog.org.uk

Swedish Church Office
6 Harcourt Street
London
W1H 2BH

Swiss Church
79 Endell Street
London
WC2H 9AJ

Tower Hamlets Local Studies Library
277 Bancroft Road
London
E1 4DQ
www.ideastore.co.uk (then click on 'Local History')

Overseas Record Offices, Societies and Museums

France

Archives Nationales
www.archivesnationales.culture.gouv.fr
The main centre is currently located in Le Marais in the centre of Paris, but a new repository is being built in Pierrefitte-sur-Seine, in the northern suburbs of Paris, which will become the main centre of the Archives Nationales from 2012. The central Paris premises will hold only pre-French Revolution records, which are those that will be of interest to those researching Huguenots. It also contains the archives of all the Parisian solicitors, which date back to the fifteenth century, and some records from the region around Paris. It should be noted that all the Parisian church registers were destroyed in 1871 during the events of the Paris commune.

La Société de L'Histoire du Protestantisme Français et Service de Généalogie (Society of the History of French Protestantism and Genealogy Service)
54 rue des Saints-Pères
Paris 75007
www.shpf.fr/
This organisation produces Les Cahiers de généalogie (Genealogy Notebooks) which cover church registers, family documents, etc., mainly from the nineteenth century.

Institute Protestant de Théologie (Protestant Institute of Theology)
83 Boulevard Arago

75014 Paris
www.iptheologie.fr

Regional museums in France

There are a number of Huguenot museums in France. A good start is Le Musée Virtuel du Protestantisme Français (the Virtual Museum of French Protestantism) at www.museeprotestant.org. This site, based in Paris, has numerous reference sources, images and a bibliography, as well as descriptions of all the Protestant museums in France. It has an English version.

Belgium

Géniwal (Généalogie Informatique Wallonie) (Walloon Genealogy Information) website in French
www.geniwal.info

Société Royale d'Histoire du protestantisme Belge (Royal Society of the History of Belgian Protestantism)
Av. Adolphe Lacomblé 60/12
B-1030 Bruxelles
www.protestanet.be/Histoire/SocRoyProt.htm

Vlaamse Vereniging voor Familiekunde (Flemish Society for Genealogy)
www.familiekunde-vlaanderen.be

Netherlands

Centraal Bureau voor Genealogie (Central Bureau of Genealogy)
Prince Willen-Alexanderhof 22
2595 BE's-Gravenhage
Post Office Box numer 11755
2502 AR's-Gravenhage
www.cbg.nl
An English-language brochure on tracing ancestors in the Netherlands, including using the Walloon Card Index, can be found on the website.

Nederlandse Hugenote Stichting (Dutch Huguenot Society)
Zacharias Jansestraat 13
1097 CH Amsterdam
www.members.chello.nl/~a.w.slager/html/huguenot.html
This society has existed since 1975 to study the history of Walloon refugees from the southern Dutch provinces of the sixteenth century and Huguenots, mainly from seventeenth-century France.

Bibliotheque Wallonne
Universiteitbibliotheek
Postbus 9501
NL-2300 RA Leiden
The Netherlands
www.library.leiden.edu
This is a central repository for the Acts of the Consistories of the Walloon
churches. There is a card index of refugees.

Germany

Deutsches Hugenottenmusem (German Huguenot Museum)
Hafenplatz 9a
34385 Bad Karlshafen
www.hugenottenmuseum.de

Deutsche Hugenotten Gesellschaft (German Huguenot Association)
www.hugenotten.de

The German Huguenot Museum of Bad Karlshafen documents the town's
foundation by Calvinists who had fled persecution in France. For Huguenot
descendants there are immigration lists and copies of church registers as
well as special literature and microfilms available for research on site, which
is also the headquarters of the German Huguenot Association.

Switzerland

International Museum of the Reformation
4 rue due Cloitre
CH-1204 Geneva
www.musee-reforme.ch

South Africa

Huguenot Memorial Museum
PO Box 37
Franschhoek

Other Huguenot Family History Societies

Australia

Huguenot Society of Australia
P.O. Box 184

Newtown
NSW 2042
www.members.optushome.com.au/ozhug

Huguenot Society of South Australia Inc
4/16 Payneham South
SA 5070
Email: bouchcom@ozemail.com.au

Huguenot Society of South Australia
15 Sandalwood Drive
St Agnes
SA 5097
Australia
E-mail: rmy15@bigpond.com

Canada

The Huguenot Society of Canada closed in 2003.

Denmark

Det Danske Huguenot Samfund
Graesager 412
DK-2980 Kokkedal
www.koudal.eu/dhs (note the website is only in Danish)

USA

The Huguenot Society of America
122 East 58th Street
New York
N.Y. 10022

The National Huguenot Society
2915 Burnside Drive
San Antonio
TX 78209-3012
www.huguenot.netnation.com

The National Huguenot Society has a number of local sections in various
American states.

INDEX

Page numbers for illustrations are given in *italics*. Towns and cities in England are listed under the county in which they are located. Other towns and cities appear under the country. There are sometime multiple entries on the same page.